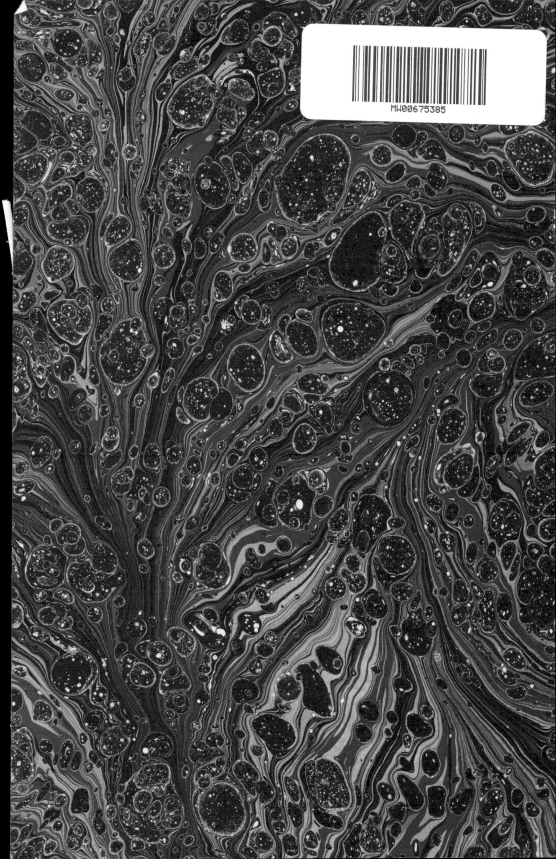

SHOULDER SLEEVE INSIGNIA
OF THE AEF

SHOULDER SLEEVE INSIGNIA

OF THE

AMERICAN EXPEDITIONARY FORCES

1918-1919

AUTHORIZED BY APPROVAL OF
GENERAL HEADQUARTERS,
AMERICAN EXPEDITIONARY FORCES

BY ORDER OF
General John J. Pershing,
Commander-in-Chief

H. Ross Ford

Schiffer Military History
Atglen, PA

Book Design by Ian Robertson.

Printed in China.
ISBN: 978-0-7643-4044-4

We are interested in hearing from authors with book ideas on related topics.

Published by Schiffer Publishing Ltd.
4880 Lower Valley Road
Atglen, PA 19310
Phone: (610) 593-1777
FAX: (610) 593-2002
E-mail: Info@schifferbooks.com.
Visit our web site at: www.schifferbooks.com
Please write for a free catalog.
This book may be purchased from the publisher.
Try your bookstore first.

In Europe, Schiffer books are distributed by:
Bushwood Books
6 Marksbury Avenue
Kew Gardens
Surrey TW9 4JF, England
Phone: 44 (0) 20 8392-8585
FAX: 44 (0) 20 8392-9876
E-mail: Info@bushwoodbooks.co.uk.
Visit our website at: www.bushwoodbooks.co.uk

Contents

Twenty-Ninth Division
Thirtieth Division
Thirty-First Division
Thirty-Second Division
Thirty-Third Division
Thirty-Fourth Division
Thirty-Fifth Division
Thirty-Sixth Division
Thirty-Seventh Division
Thirty-Eighth Division
Thirty-Ninth Division
Fortieth Division
Forty-First Division
Forty-Second Division
Seventy-Sixth Division
Seventy-Seventh Division
Seventy-Eighth Division
Seventy-Ninth Division
Eightieth Division
Eighty-First Division
Eighty-Second Division
Eighty-Third Division
Eighty-Fourth Division
Eighty-Fifth Division
Eighty-Sixth Division
Eighty-Seventh Division
Eighty-Eighth Division
Eighty-Ninth Division
Ninetieth Division
Ninety-First Division
Ninety-Second Division
Ninety-Third Division (Provisional)

Preface

As a collector of U.S. military shoulder sleeve insignia (SSI) since 1941, I undertook writing this publication recognizing that, to my knowledge, there was no definitive source dealing solely with the authorized SSI of the World War I era. It was not until 1918, just over 90 years ago, that SSI were authorized to be worn by units serving in the American Expeditionary Forces, both U.S. Army and U.S. Marine Corps. This publication is the result of my quest to identify all the officially authorized shoulder sleeve insignia of the U.S. Army, Army Reserve, and Army National Guard, as well as U.S. Navy and U.S. Marine Corps from World War I to date.

That quest began in earnest after I introduced my digital database "Master Patch Guide" covering the SSI of the U.S. Army, Army Reserve, and Army National Guard at the American Society of Military Insignia Collectors (ASMIC) 2006 Convention and annual meeting. My discussions with fellow collectors revealed that to date no "publication" had definitely depicted all the officially approved SSI since the inception thereof in 1918. I thus decided to undertake that task.

In that quest I have conducted extensive research at the National Archives and The Institute of Heraldry, and have appreciated the cooperation of The Army Historical Society, the U.S. Army Heritage & Education Center, the World War I Museum, the Quartermaster Museum, others and, of course, the American Society of Military Insignia Collectors, of which I have been a member for almost five decades. It has been a challenging quest. In 2007 a second edition of "Master Patch Guide" was published, including what I then believed were *all* of the then known verified authorized SSI of the U.S. Army, Army Reserve, and Army National Guard (visit masterpatchguide.com). I have subsequently continued to add newly authorized SSI, and have added numerous WWI era insignia that have been verified as approved through subsequent research.

The first consideration in researching the approved shoulder sleeve insignia of the WWI era was recognition that the authorized approving authority was the General Headquarters, American Expeditionary Forces, the headquarters of General John J.

Pershing, Commander-in-Chief. I note this because, as my investigation confirmed, there were many insignia worn that were not approved by the appropriate authority and thus not "authorized." Some of those were worn by troops at their own discretion and others by the approval of subordinate commands, such as Army, Corps, Division, and various other unit commanders. As in my "Master Patch Guide" and this publication, I will deal only with the authorized - officially approved - SSI. However, in certain instances I will comment on other commonly worn variations of approved insignia or designs known to have been worn in the period or by troops returning to the U.S. post war.

Over the past several years I have reviewed tens of thousands of records relating to the authorization of SSI, especially those from the WWI era of the American Expeditionary Forces. I have copied several thousand pages to authenticate information relating to the approvals and to assure quotations there from are accurately restated herein. In that regard I have reflected the use of upper and lower case in quotations as well as misspellings, etc., based on the materials I have on file. In an effort to conserve some repetitiveness, references to General Headquarters, American Expeditionary Forces (G.H.Q., A.E.F.) for approvals and other communications are "By command of General Pershing" and signed by "The Adjutant General".

The vast majority of the materials (both documents and pictorial) utilized in this publication are from the records of the National Archives or The Institute of Heraldry. Also, references for unit lineages and campaign credits are from material published in the Army Historical Series, "American Military History"; the Army Lineage Series of the U.S. Army Center of Military History; and the Center's republication of the "United States Army in the World War, 1917-1919."

The most significant difference between this publication and those that have depicted many insignia samples of the WWI era is that herein most of the pictured images are copies of the actual drawings, prints, paintings, and in some cases sample SSI that are in the official approval records of the American Expeditionary Forces. However, in some cases sketches have been prepared based on the approved descriptions in order to illustrate those for which official pictorial material was not found of record.

H. Ross Ford
Williamsburg, Virginia
2012

Acknowledgments

Thirty-eight years ago, in 1973 our fellow American Society of Military Insignia Collectors (ASMIC) members, the late Wm. Edgar Goodman, Jr., and Mark M. Hough authored four articles on World War I era shoulder sleeve insignia of the U.S. Army in the society's quarterly *Trading Post*. Those articles were written based on the research of the National Archives by Mark during his residency in the Washington, D.C. area and the extensive shoulder sleeve insignia collection and knowledge of Edgar Goodman. I knew and visited with Edgar in the 1960s, and Mark was helpful to me as I undertook this project. I also want to acknowledge the article "The Origins of the Army Shoulder Patch" by fellow ASMIC member Patrick D. McLaughlin in the July-September 1983 *Trading Post*, and certainly others who have contributed articles relating to the WWI era distinctive cloth designs worn on the uniform. I especially appreciate the assistance of the research staffs of the National Archives and of The Institute of Heraldry, without whose cooperative help this publication would not have been possible. I also want to acknowledge Mitchell A. Yockelson of the National Archives (author of *Borrowed Soldiers Americans Under British Command, 1918* ISBN-13: 978-008061-3919-7) for his help over the past several years.

I also appreciate the assistance of fellow collectors David Johnson (Colonel, U.S. Army retired) and Steve Johnson ("The Johnson Brothers") for allowing me to review their extensive collection of WWI era insignia, and for their helpful review of my manuscript. Most important I thank my dear wife of over 50 years, Louisa, who has been a great supporter, typist, and editor as we have prepared the book for publication.

Background
United States Involvement in WWI

When on 3 June 1916 the National Defense Act of 1916 was signed into law, "The Great War" – World War I – that had commenced in the early days of August 1914 continued to go badly for the Allies in Europe; U.S. citizens had been killed in German U-boat attacks and Pancho Villa had crossed into New Mexico and shot up the town of Columbus. The act authorized an increase in the peace time strength of the Regular Army to 175,000 men, a wartime strength of close to 300,000, and authorized 117 regiments, of which 65 were infantry regiments; increased the National Guard four-fold to a strength of 400,000; established a Volunteer Army to be raised in time of war (later renamed the National Army); and established the Reserve Officers' Training Corps.

Although the organizational structure of divisions was still in question, the War Department decided to immediately form 32 divisions: 16 in the National Guard and 16 in the National Army. As the war in Europe continued its heavy toll on Allied forces, the commencement of the Russian revolution in March, and learning that Germany was negotiating with Mexico to join its camp, on 6 April 1917 the United States declared war on Germany. At the time, the Regular Army numbered less than 135,000 and there were no complete units larger than regiments. A month later on 18 May the Selective Service Act of 1917 passed Congress and provided a broad structure for the Army: (1) the Regular Army, to be raised to 286,000; (2) the National Guard expanded to approximately 450,000; and (3) the National Army created in two increments of 500,000 each at the President's determination.

By letter of the Secretary of War, Newton D. Baker, of 26 May 1917 transmitting Presidential instructions, Major General John J. Pershing was appointed Commander-in-Chief of the American Expeditionary Forces, and by General Orders No. 1 the Headquarters, American Expeditionary Forces was formed. Shortly after his arrival in France on 13 June, General Pershing recommended to the War Department that every effort should be made to have 1,000,000 soldiers in France by May 1918 serving in 20 divisions and supporting services, and that plans should be made to eventually have 3,000,000 American troops in the field in Europe. General Pershing and staff then undertook a General Organization Project, and in July reported to the War Department that the army should be organized in divisions of approximately 25,000 troops and outlined their structure. The War Department, using the General Organization Project recommendation as a basis, determined the division structure would consist of 2 infantry brigades of 2 regiments; 3 machine gun battalions; a field artillery brigade with 1 heavy and 2 light regiments; a regiment of combat engineers; a signal battalion; and supporting trains. In June 1918 General Pershing increased his estimate of troops to 3,000,000 with 66 divisions in France by May 1919, and shortly thereafter increased the estimate to 80 divisions, and by July 1919 100 divisions.

To form the first Regular Army division, 1st Expeditionary Division, General Pershing nominated the 16th, 18th, 26th, and 28th Infantry and the 6th Field Artillery regiments.

In the summer of 1917, the War Department designated that Regular Army divisions would be numbered 1 through 25; National Guard 26 through 75 (several National Guard divisions were renumbered to conform); and National Army 76 and higher.

At the time of America's entry into the war, the only identifying insignia in use for U.S. Army units was the addition of numerals and/or letters affixed to the unit's branch insignia and worn on the standing collar of the uniform blouse. For example, the crossed rifles of the infantry might display a numeral for the regiment's designation above and sometimes a letter below to identify the company.

The organization of General Headquarters, American Expeditionary Forces was established by General Orders No. 8 of 5 July 1917, and consisted of the Commander-in-Chief; chief of staff; general staff; secretary of the general staff; and administrative and technical staff, including logistical functions. General Headquarters was initially located in Paris, relocated to Chaumont 13 September 1917, and then back to Paris 12 July 1919. By General Orders No. 88 of 22 August 1919, General Headquarters was transferred to Washington, D.C. effective 1 September 1919, and by War Department General Orders No. 49 of 14 August 1920, General Headquarters, American Expeditionary Forces was abolished effective 31 August 1920. General Pershing was promoted to the rank of General of the Armies by Act of Congress in September 1919. He became Chief of Staff of the Army 1 July 1921, serving to his retirement 13 September 1924. General Pershing died 15 July 1948 at age 87.

General John J. Pershing, France, October 1918.
Records of the National Archives.

General Pershing Army Chief of Staff, by
Richard Leopold Seyffert. The Army Art
Collection, Center of Military History.

Deployment of Divisions to France

Division	Dates of Movement Oversea	Remarks
1st	June-December 1917	
2d	September 1917-March 1918	Organized in France
3d	March-June 1918	
4th	May-June 1918	British shipping program
5th	March-June 1918	
6th	June-July 1918	
7th	July-September 1918	
8th	November 1918	Headquarters only
26th	September 1917-January 1918	
27th	May-July 1918	British shipping program
28th	April-June 1918	British shipping program
29th	June-July 1918	
30th	May-June 1918	British shipping program
31st	September-November 1918	Skeletonized
32d	January-March 1918	
33d	May-June 1918	British shipping program
34th	September-October 1918	Skeletonized
35th	April-June 1918	British shipping program
36th	July-August 1918	
37th	June-July 1918	
38th	September-October 1918	Skeletonized
39th	August-September 1918	Depot, later Skeletonized
40th	July-September 1918	Depot
41st	November 1917-February 1918	Depot
42d	October-December 1917	
76th	July-August 1918	Depot
77th	March-May 1918	British shipping program
78th	May-June 1918	British shipping program
79th	July-August 1918	
80th	May-June 1918	British shipping program
81st	July-August 1918	
82d	April-July 1918	British shipping program
83d	June-August 1918	Depot
84th	August-October 1918	Depot, later Skeletonized
85th	July-August 1918	Depot
86th	September-October 1918	Skeletonized
87th	June-September 1918	Broken up for laborers
88th	August-September 1918	
89th	June-July 1918	
90th	June-July 1918	
91st	June-July 1918	
92d	June-July 1918	
93d	December 1917-April 1918	Provisional unit, discontinued May 1918

Demobilization of Divisions

Division	Returned to U.S.	Demobilized	Camp/Location
1st	September 1919		Zachary Taylor, Kentucky
2d	August 1919		Travis, Texas
3d	August 1919		Pike, Arkansas
4th	August 1919		Dodge, Iowa
5th	July 1919		Gordon, Georgia
6th	June 1919		Grant, Illinois
7th	June 1919		Funston, Kansas
8th*	September 1919	September 1919	Dix, New Jersey
9th	#	February 1919	Sheridan, Alabama
10th	#	February 1919	Funston, Kansas
11th	#	February 1919	Meade, Maryland
12th	#	February 1919	Devens, Massachusetts
13th	#	March 1919	Lewis, Washington
14th	#	February 1919	Custer, Michigan
15th	#	February 1919	Logan, Texas
16th	#	March 1919	Kearny, California
17th	#	February 1919	Beauregard, Louisiana
18th	#	February 1919	Travis, Texas
19th	#	February 1919	Dodge, Iowa
20th	#	February 1919	Sevier, South Carolina
26th	April 1919	May 1919	Devens, Massachusetts
27th	March 1919	April 1919	Upton, New York
28th	April 1919	May 1919	Dix, New Jersey
29th	May 1919	May 1919	Dix, New Jersey
30th	April 1919	May 1919	Jackson, South Carolina
31st	December 1918	January 1919	Gordon, Georgia
32d	May 1919	May 1919	Custer, Michigan
33d	May 1919	June 1919	Grant, Illinois
34th	January 1919	February 1919	Grant, Illinois
35th	April 1919	May 1919	Funston, Kansas
36th	June 1919	June 1919	Bowie, Texas
37th	April 1919	June 1919	Sherman, Ohio
38th	December 1918	January 1919	Zachary Taylor, Kentucky
39th	December 1918	January 1919	Beauregard, Louisiana
40th	March 1919	April 1919	Kearny, California
41st	February 1919	February 1919	Dix, New Jersey
42d	May 1919	May 1919	Dix, New Jersey
76th	December 1918	January 1919	Devens, Massachusetts
77th	April 1919	May 1919	Upton, New York
78th	June 1919	June 1919	Dix, New Jersey
79th	May 1919	June 1919	Dix, New Jersey
80th	May 1919	June 1919	Lee, Virginia
81st	June 1919	June 1919	Hoboken, New Jersey

82d	May 1919	May 1919	Upton, New York
83d	January 1919	October 1919	Sherman, Ohio
84th	January 1919	July 1919	Zachary Taylor, Kentucky
85th	March 1919	April 1919	Custer, Michigan
86th	January 1919	January 1919	Grant, Illinois
87th	January 1919	February 1919	Dix, New Jersey
88th	June 1919	June 1919	Dodge, Iowa
89th	May 1919	July 1919	Funston, Kansas
90th	June 1919	June 1919	Bowie, Texas
91st	April 1919	May 1919	Presidio of San Francisco, California
92d	February 1919	February 1919	Meade, Maryland
93d	@		
95th	#	December 1919	Sherman, Ohio
96th	#	January 1919	Wadsworth, New York
97th	#	December 1918	Cody, New Mexico
98th	#	November 1918	McClellan, Alabama
99th	#	November 1918	Wheeler, Georgia
100th	#	November 1918	Bowie, Texas
101st	#	November 1918	Shelby, Mississippi
102d	#	November 1918	Dix, New Jersey

Notes:

* Only part of the division overseas.

Did not go overseas. (Not considered divisions of the American Expeditionary Forces.)

@ Provisional division, headquarters demobilized in France in May 1918.

Origin and Evolution
of Shoulder Sleeve Insignia
World War I

Although I know many readers know the "origin" of the wearing of shoulder sleeve insignia by the U.S. Army, I will briefly comment thereon for those who may not. It is generally accepted that the origin of the U.S. Army adopting the wearing of shoulder sleeve insignia is credited to the 81st Division's commanding general, Major General Charles J. Bailey. Having observed British and French units wearing distinguishing "patches" during a visit to the battlefront in France in early 1918, he suggested to his staff that a design for a 81st Division patch be developed. The division was in training at Wildcat Creek, Fort Jackson, South Carolina, at the time, and the suggested wildcat design was adopted. General Bailey, not waiting for any approvals, ordered patches made for the division whose troops were headed for the New York Port of Embarkation at Hoboken, New Jersey. On 1 August 1918 the 81st sailed for France, and en route General Bailey ordered the troops to sew the patches on their uniforms. Subsequent to their arrival in France the wearing of the patches was noted, and upon being advised General Pershing ordered that the "unauthorized" patches were to be removed. General Bailey personally protested the decision on the basis that the British and French forces wore distinguishing marks, and that they provided officers the ability to distinguish their troops and improved esprit de corps. More importantly, he argued that to remove the insignia would cause a loss in morale to the division. General Pershing relented and is reported to have said, "All right, go ahead and wear it. And see to it that you live up to it." The official approval of the 81st wildcat SSI was sent by a telegram of 19 October 1918 from G.H.Q., A.E.F.

On 15 October 1918 a memorandum was issued by the Chief of Staff, American Expeditionary Forces, to the Adjutant General, stating:

"The Commander-in-Chief directs that a telegram substantially as follows be sent to Army Commanders and the Commanding Generals of all Divisions now serving with American Armies:

Each Division will adopt and procure immediately some distinctive cloth design which will be worn by every officer and man of the Division on the left arm, the upper part to be attached to the shoulder sleeve. Report will be made to these Headquarters by telegram as to designs adopted and in order that there may be no duplication approval of design will be made by telegram from these Headquarters."

On 19 October 1918 G.H.Q., A.E.F., by telegram ordered all Division commanders:

"NUMBER M-674 EACH DIVISION WILL ADOPT AND PROCURE IMMEDIATELY SOME DISTINCTIVE CLOTH DESIGN WHICH WILL BE WORN BY EVERY OFFICER AND MAN OF THE DIVISION ON THE LEFT ARM COMMA THE UPPER PART TO BE ATTACHED TO THE SHOULDER SEAM PERIOD REPORT WILL BE MADE TO THESE HEADQUARTERS BY TELEGRAM AS TO DESIGNS ADOPTED AND IN ORDER THAT THERE MAY BE NO DUPLICATION APPROVAL OF DESIGN WILL BE MADE BY TELEGRAM FROM THESE HEADQUARTERS."

Subsequently, the order was broadened to include the Armies and Corps. Units began immediately to submit designs by description, sketch or sample. Many were promptly approved, some redesigned, and some rejected as inappropriate, or the unit not qualifying for a separate distinguishing insignia. G.H.Q., A.E.F. granted approvals from 19 October 1918 through the second quarter of 1919. (Although the armistice was declared 11 November 1918, units of the American Expeditionary Forces and Third Army remained in the theater in occupational duties until the last thousand troops left for home on 24 January 1923.)

The 81st Division (Wildcat design) was the first SSI approved by telegram M-681 by order of General Pershing 19 October 1918. The 28th Division (red Keystone design) was approved by telegram M-682 of the same date.

Within 5 days SSI had been approved for 16 divisions, and by 1 September 1919, when G.H.Q., A.E.F. relocated to Washington, D.C. 193 insignia, including verified approved variations, had been authorized for units of 80 primary U.S. Army and Marine Corps organizations.

On 24 October 1918 G.H.Q., A.E.F. issued a MEMORANDUM for Col. Walter S Grant, Deputy Chief of Staff, 1st Army:

"Following is a list of the Divisions which have submitted descriptions of distinctive design adopted, and which have been approved by this office, with a brief description of the design in each case:

1st Division.	Red figure "1" about 5 inches high.
3rd Division.	Royal blue cloth 2 ¼ inches square, having diagonally across it 3 white stripes 5/16 inches wide and 5/16 inches apart.
5th Division.	Red diamond.
6th Division.	Six pointed star.
7th Division.	Two black equilateral triangles with a base of 3 cm. superimposed upon a red circle with a diameter of 6 cm; the base of 1 triangle is horizontal, with the apexes of the base angles resting on the circumference of the circle, the second triangle inverted with the base parallel to the base of the first; an imaginary line bisecting the bases of both triangles would pass thru their apexes and make the vertical diameter of the circle.
28th Division.	Red Keystone.
29th Division.	Korean lucky symbol, same as trademark used by Northern Pacific Railway.
30th Division.	Monogram, letter "O" surrounding letter "H", with three "X"s inside the cross-bar of the "H"; on maroon cloth. OH stands for Old Hickory, and the three Xs for 30th.
33d Division.	Yellow cross on a black circular background 2 in. in diameter.
77th Division.	Gold Statue of Liberty 2 ¼ in. high, on blue background 2 ½ in. high; width at top 1 in., at bottom 2 in.
78th Division.	Red semicircle, 3 in. in diameter, to be worn circumference on top.
80th Division.	Division shield 2 ¼ in. broad and deep, made of olive-drab cloth and bearing superimposed in center 3 blue hills ¾ in. high, all outlined in white, symbolical of States of Virginia, West Virginia and Pennsylvania.
81st Division.	Wild cat.
82d Division.	Square red cloth, blue disk superimposed.
88th Division.	Two figures "8" crossing at right angles to each other giving the appearance of a Maltese cross made of loops.
92d Division.	Buffalo."

On 2 November by 1st Ind. G.H.Q., American E.F. to Col. W. S. Grant, Deputy Chief of Staff, 1st Army wrote:

"No designs of insignia have yet been approved for the 32d, 79th and 36th Divisions. The approved designs of the other divisions mentioned are as follows:

2d Division.	5 pointed white star with blue Indian head superimposed; cloth background of different colors to designate the several organizations.
89th Division.	Black letter "W" in circle.
26th Division.	Monogram letters "Y D."
90th Division.	Monogram letters "T O""

On 9 November 1918 HEADQUARTERS FIRST ARMY issued GENERAL ORDERS No. 33 as follows:

"I.   The following designs of distinctive insignia, to be worn on the left shoulder with the top of the insignia at the shoulder seam of sleeve of coat, have been approved for Army Troops, First Army, and the Corps and Divisions named hereafter, and are published for the information of all concerned:

First Army	A Block Letter "A" of black cloth 4 inches long, 3 inches wide at top.
I Corps	White circle on a dark blue back ground.
III Corps	Three pointed star of light blue cloth.
V Corps	A Pentagon with cream colored spokes running from each corner to the Center."

(The Division descriptions were essentially the same as the 24 October memorandum and 2 November 1st Ind. heretofore cited.)

GENERAL ORDERS No. 33 continued:

"Pending the receipt of these insignia upon requisition, the Commanding Generals of the Corps named above, and the commanding Generals of each of the Divisions as may pertain to the 1st Army, will at once take the necessary steps to provide their troops with their particular insignia. As cloth of the prescribed color may not be readily available a temporary expedient will be adopted by using khaki or olive-drab cloth, or some other colored cloth, cut according to pattern."

"All officers and men pertaining to the above Corps and to the Divisions now pertaining to the 1st Army will have the authorized insignia of the proper shape and of as uniform a color as possible, on their uniform by November 20th. After that date all men found without it will be arrested as stragglers, unless they are in a detachment under the control of a responsible officer."

Clearly, the sentence of General Orders No. 33 attests as to why some confusion exists as to the colors of some of the initially authorized insignia:

"As cloth of the prescribed color may not be readily available a temporary expedient will be adopted by using khaki or olive-drab cloth, or some other colored cloth, cut according to pattern."

Therefore, when descriptions or samples were requested from the Chief Quartermaster, 1ˢᵗ Army, some depicted olive-drab in place of the intended color.

Subsequently G.H.Q., A.E.F. approved numerous other unit insignia as set forth hereinafter under the unit designations.

Office Chief Q.M. AEF on January 1, 1919 issued:

"LIST OF DIVISIONAL INSIGNIAS APPROVED BY GHQ TO DATE.

1ˢᵗ Div.	Oblong chevron of O.D. Cloth, approximately 2-3/4 inches wide and 3-3/4 inches long all over, which is cut away at the end to form a point whose sides enclose an angle of 90 degrees. Upon the Chevron and in the center, is imposed a figure "1", 1 ¾ inches high, made of crimson cloth.
2ⁿᵈ Div.	Indian head stamped on a 5-pointed star of white cloth, with background for star of cloth of different colors to designate several organizations of the division.
3ʳᵈ Div.	Patch of royal blue cloth 2-1/4 inches square, having diagonally across it 3 white stripes 5/16 inches wide and 5/16 inches apart.
4ᵗʰ Div.	4 Ivy leaves placed in cross shape about small circle; color, green.
5ᵗʰ Div.	Diamond of red cloth, 3 inches long, 2 inches wide.
6ᵗʰ Div.	Six pointed star of red cloth, with blue figure "6" superimposed.
7ᵗʰ Div.	Two black equilateral triangles with base of 3 cm. superimposed upon a red circle with a diameter of 6 cm. The base of one triangle is horizontal, with the apexes of the base angles resting on the circumference of the circle, the second triangle inverted with the base parallel to the base of the first. An imaginary line bisecting the bases of both triangles would pass through their apexes and make the vertical diameter of the circle.
26ᵗʰ Div.	Letters "YD" in monogram, in blue cloth, color of French uniform.
27ᵗʰ Div.	Black circle with red border and several stars and peculiar design superimposed.
28ᵗʰ. Div.	Keystone of red cloth.

29th Div.	Korean lucky symbol; colors, blue and gray (same as trade mark of Northern Pacific Ry.)
30th Div.	Elliptical maroon cloth 2-3/4 inches by 1-3/4 inches, with blue border, making letter "O" with letter "H" of blue cloth in center; Inside the cross bar of letter "H" are three figures "X"
32nd Div.	Red arrow with cross bar in center.
33rd Div.	Yellow cross on black circular background, 2 inches in diameter.
34th Div.	Skull of steer with horns, front view, made of red cloth sewed on oval patch of black cloth.
35th Div.	Santa Fe cross, indifferent colors for different units.
36th Div.	Khaki disk, 3-5/8 in. in diameter, with blue arrow head superimposed. Arrowhead 2-1/4 X 3-1/16 in. including neck of arrow which is 1 in. x 3/4 in. Letter "T" within the arrowhead, 1-3/16 X 3/4 inches. Color of "T" khaki.
37th Div.	Red circle 1-1/2 inches in diameter with white border 3/8" wide.
38th Div.	Shield 2" wide by 2" long, left half Navy blue, right half artillery red. Superimposed in exact center of shiled a white initial letter "C", 1 inch vertical x 1 inch transverse, with small letter vertical "y" interlaced with lower limb of initial "C". Letters in white.
40th Div.	Sun with 12 ray points embroidered in golden yellow on a sky blue patch, emblematic of the "Sunshine Division". Dimensitons blue patch 3" X 3". Sun – diameter of circle 1"; diameter including rays to be 2 inches.
42nd Div.	1 inch quarter circle band of which radius of outer edge 1-3/4 inches. This band composed of 3 colored bands each 1/3 in. wide. Colors: Blue, yellow and red; the latter being outside color.
77th Div.	Liberty Statue 2-1/4" high in gold on blue back ground 2-1/2 inches high; width at top 1", at bottom 2". Figure to be cut from gold cloth and applied on blue background.
78th Div.	Red semicircle 3" in diameter; circumference on top.
79th Div.	Gray Lorrain Cross on blue shield; Base patch: Gray, ashield 2-1/2 inch wide at top and 2-5/8" high. Cut out patch: Blue, a shield 2-3/8 inch wide at top and 2-1/2 inches high, and inclosing a cut out Lorrain cross 2-3/8 inch high with arms 1/4 inch thick and 1-3/8 inch and 1-1/2 inch long.

80th Div.	Shield 2-1/4 inches broad and deep made of olive drab cloth and bearing superimposed in center 3 blue hills 3/4" high; all outlined in white.
81st Div.	Wild cat; different colored cats for different branches of the service.
82nd Div.	Square of red cloth, 6 cms by 6 cms with red circle of blue cloth superimposed, centers coincident. Blue circle to be 4.5 cms in diameter and sewed to the red background.
84th Div.	Red Hatchet.
85th Div.	Scarlet cloth mounted on a circle of O.D. cloth 1/4" larger than the design.
86th Div.	Red shield with black eagle with superimposed red shield and initials "BH"
87th Div.	Patch of green cloth, form of circle, flattened at top for sewing to shoulder seam, 2-1/2" in dia. and having in center of this field an acorn made of brown cloth.
88th Div.	2 elongated figures "8" crossing at right angles to each other, giving the appearance of a Maltese Cross made of loops.
89th Div.	Black letter "W" in circle
90th Div.	Monogram letters "TO"
91st Div.	Pine tree cut from Green cloth inscribed in a triangle, the base of which is 2" and the altitude 2" with a trunk 1/2 inch long and 1/4" wide.
92nd Div.	Buffalo

CORPS DESIGNS

1ST Corps	White circle on O.D. background. Greater diameter 8 cm inner diameter 6 cm.
3rd Corps	Equilateral Triangle, sides of 2.30 cms. 3 Isosceles triangles base 2.30 cms with altitude of 4 cms. Color light blue.
5th Corps	Pentagon with cream colored side and spokes running from each corner to the center. Olive drab background. Radius to each point 5 cms. Width of spokes and outside 1 cm.
7th Corps	White figure "7" on a shield of colbat blue, to be sewed on a patch of khaki, 5-1/2 cm square.
8th Corps	Octagonal in shape and composed ofa blue field, blue as in the US flag, bearing a white 8, and a white border around the edge, to conform to the following spec. Maximum dia of insignia 2", white border around the edge to be 1/16" wide. The 8 to be

octagonal in shape and is to be centered with the sides parallel to the sides of the insignia, the max. diameter of the bottom part of the eight to be 7/8", the max. diameter of the top of the 8 to be 3/4". The line forming the 8 to be 1/8" wide

9th Corps
Red circular band 3/8" wide, with outer diameter of 2-1/2 inches, inclosing IX of like dimensions, all superimposed on a Prussian Blue circle, three inches in diameter.

ARMY INSIGIAS

1ST Army.
Block letter "A" black cloth, base 3 inches, altitude 4 inches; sides, top and crossbar 1/4 inch thick.

2nd Army.
Figure "2" blocked; base 40 mm. altitude 50 mm; upper half red, lower half white.

GHQ Insignia
A circle of red, white and blue bands is being made. This is not yet finally approved."

On 25 January 1919 WAR DEPARTMENT issued Circular No. 42, on the subject of the wearing of "Divisional Insignia" upon return to the United States as follows:

"Circular No. 18, War Department, 1919, is rescinded and the following substituted therefore:

Officers and enlisted men returning from France as casuals for the purpose of discharge, will be permitted to wear insignia indicating the tactical division, Army Corps or Army with which they served overseas. This applies not only to those who are to be immediately discharged but also to those retained in hospitals pending discharge.

Officers and enlisted men returning as casuals not for discharge but for active duty in this country will be required to remove such insignia.

Units returning from overseas for the purpose of demobilization will be permitted to wear divisional, Army Corps or Army insignia until demobilized. Units returning for station in this country, which are not to be demobilized will be required to remove such insignia."

(A complete copy of War Department Circular No. 42 1919 was not found in the records reviewed. Thus, the above is believed to be an excerpt there from.)

In a communication from GENERAL HEADQUARTERS AMERICAN EXPEDITIONARY FORCES INTELLIGENCE SECTION of 17 February 1919, O.I.C., Photographic Sub-section, G-2-D to Chief, G-2-D, G.H.Q., A.E.F. wrote:

"1. In order to provide the historical archives with proper photographic records of the various shoulder badges used in the A.E.F., I recently obtained from Depot Quartermaster,

Paris, samples of all shoulder badges he had in stock and have had them photographed and painted in colors at the Signal Corps Photographic Laboratory, Vincennes. The number of shoulder badges obtained from the Depot Quartermaster and the units they designate follow: 30th Division; 27th Division; Ambulance Service; two of the 8th Army Corps; 2nd Army Corps; 26th Division; 1st Division; 29th Division; 42nd Division; 80th Division; 78th Division; 79th Division; 36th Division; 7th Army Corps; 77th Division; six of the 81st Division; fifteen of the First Army; 9th Army Corps; 303rd Field Artillery; 85th Division; 4th Army Corps; 33rd Division; 7th Division; 3rd Army Corps; 1st Army Corps; 82nd Division; 37th Division; 35th Division; 6th Army Corps; 5th Army Corps; 89th Division; 5th Division; 28th Division; 84th Division; These do not include all of the shoulder badges authorized and worn in the A.E.F. It is requested that samples of all others, aside from those named above, be obtained and forwarded to this office in order that they may be photographed for the historical records. 2. It is requested that the official description of each of these shoulder badges, inclusive of those listed above, be obtained and forwarded to this office for use as titles or captions to accompany the photographs and paintings. 3. Attention is invited to the fact that the shoulder badge for the same unit often is in different colors; for example the shoulder badge of the 83rd, so called "Wild Cat Division", appears in five different colors. The badge of the First Army has numerous arrangement of color schemes within the principal design. These doubtless are for units within the First Army, but thus far I have not been able to obtain the proper explanations. 4. For the purpose of historical accuracy it is requested that the significance of each of the designs be stated and that in cases where units have chosen other names for themselves, other than the Divisional number, for example "Wild Cat Division", please also give these names." (Note: The reference to the 303rd Field Artillery in "1." may in fact be for the 76th Division, recognizing that the regiment was a unit assigned to the Division and that no insignia were authorized by G.H.Q., A.E.F. for regimental units. In "3." the reference to the 83rd Division is really the 81st Division, and there is no verifying evidence that the variations of the 1st Army insignia were approved by G.H.Q., A.E.F.)

In response, on 20 February Acting Chief, G-2-D wrote:

"This memorandum is in reply to your letter on the subject of shoulder insignia. This department made a request a short time ago for samples and drawings in color of the Army, Corps and Divisional insignia, also the various insignia of the S.O.S., together with history of the adoption of the various insignia, nick-names etc. A few days ago the Historical Section, War Plans Division, Washington, requested that we make a similar demand for their records. These samples and drawings are now beginning to arrive in the office. In view of the difficulty and slowness of obtaining these samples, it is suggested that we hold the insignia which we are now receiving, until such time as we have a complete set, at which time it will be possible for you to make such use as may be necessary for the photographic history.

In this connection, we wish to call your attention to a chart recently prepared in color by G-2-C, which contains all insignia adopted to date.

In respect to paragraph 3, referring to the Wild Cat Division and the appearance of the insignia of that division in several colors, our information is that each color represents a different arm of service incorporated in the division. We have no samples of the insignia in all the colors, but have one insignia with a statement that this or that color represents certain branches of the service. This same rule will apply in other cases where more than one color is used to designate different branches of service."

On 19 November 1919, General Headquarters American Expeditionary Forces, then stationed in Washington, D.C., issued a Memorandum as follows:

"The insignias attached, have been carefully checked with the following results:
    1. There is no record that the following were ever submitted to Headquarters, AEF., for consideration and approval.

    10th Division
    11th Division
    12th Division
    13th Division
    14th Division
    18th Division
    19th Division
    39th Division
    40th Engineers
    56th Engineers
    American Mission Mallet Reserve
    Office of the Chief of Engineers
    Construction Engineers
    14th Railroad Transportation
    First Army Headquarters
    Motor Transport

The above may have been approved by other authority as a number of the organizations listed were not a part of the American Expeditionary Forces. They were not approved by the Commander-in-Chief, American E. F.
    2. The following were disapproved by the Commander-in-Chief, American E. F.
    (a) Oozelfinch Railway Artillery
    (b) American Forces in Italy
    (c) The request of the Railroad Transportation Corps in the AEF for separate insignia, was disapproved. No design was submitted with the request. It is not known whether the design printed is for troops in France or the United States.
    3. The following mistakes are noted.
    (a) The insignia of the 84th Division, as approved, is attached.
    (b) General Headquarters should be surrounded with circle of olive drab instead of white.
    (c) The title under SOS should be "Service of Supply" and not Base Section, Sources of Supply.
    (d) Advance Section should read "Advance Section, Service of Supply".

(e) The polar bear was the approved insignia for all of the North Russian Expeditionary Forces. The title should be "North Russian Expeditionary Force" instead of Transportation, Corps, Railway, etc."

4. Attached is the approved insignia for Educational Corps, which is not on your list. This organization was operated only a short time.

5. The insignia for the Anti-Aircraft was submitted after the organization had returned to the United States. This insignia was returned to The Adjutant General of the Army without recommendation."

Signed W.W. Carr, Adjutant General, and with a "P.S. When the corrections have been made the writer would appreciate having three or four copies of the poster"

(Note that paragraph 2. above does not include all the designs disapproved by G.H.Q., A.E.F.)

On 3 May 1920 WAR DEPARTMENT issued "Circular No. 164. SHOULDER PATCH INSIGNIA":

"1. Each Regular Army division will wear the shoulder patch insignia adopted by the division of the same numerical designation during The World War. 2. Staff corps and departments and operating services that have adopted shoulder patch insignia are authorized to wear them or in the event that insignia have not been adopted to submit designs for approval. 3. So much of Circular No. 42, War Department, 1919 (Divisional insignia), as conflicts with the provisions of this circular is rescinded. (421.7, A.G.O.) By order of the Secretary of War:"

By MEMORANDUM of 14 May 1920 the Asst. Director of Purchases and Storage of the Quartermaster corps wrote Assistant Chief of Staff, Director of Operations:

"Subject patch insignia. 1. Reference Circular #164, War Department, May 3, 1920, which authorizes the use of shoulder patch insignia, this office holds standard samples of this insignia for G.H.Q. seven regular divisions, three armies (1st, 2nd, and 3rd), nine corps (1st to 9th incl.), Tank Service and Chemical Warfare Service. 2. The circular above mentioned directs such services as have not adopted shoulder patch insignia to submit designs for same for approval and adoption. 3. It is requested that these services be directed to submit designs with quantity of each desired as soon as possible. 4. Information is also desired as to the number to be authorized per man under Circular #377, 1919, the soldier is authorized to have three coats, cotton, two coats, woolen, and one overcoat, a total of six coats. Will six shoulder patch insignia constitute the initial allowance for each soldier and will this insignia be issued gratuitously to commissioned officers or will they be required to purchase same? 5. Should any shoulder patch insignia be procured for armies and corps? 6. The information requested above is necessary to enable this office to prepare intelligent estimated and make procurement of a properly balanced stock of these insignia."

By 1ˢᵗ Ind. of 28 May 1920 War Department, A.G.O. replied:

"Circular 164, W.D., May 3, 1920 <u>directs</u> the Regular Army Divisions to wear the shoulder patch insignia but <u>authorizes</u> Corps and Services that have adopted one to wear the same or submit designs for approval. It is not mandatory for any except Regular Army Divisions under this circular.

The act of Congress approved July 11th, 1919, provides for the Chemical Warfare Service, the Air Service, the Construction Division, the Tank Corps and the Motor Transport Corps until June 30, 1920 only, and until the future of these services is determined, it is not deemed advisable at present to procure shoulder patch insignia for them.

No shoulder patch insignia will be procured for armies or corps at this time.

Three shoulder patch insignia per man will be the initial allowance under Circular 152, April 20 1920, for enlisted men.

Shoulder patch insignia for issue to troops for use on cotton uniforms will be fast color and as far as practicable on non-shrinkable material.

Officers will be required to purchase their own shoulder patch insignia.

By order of the Secretary of War."

On 5 June 1920 Chief, Equipment Branch, operations Division wrote THE CHIEF OF STAFF:

"Subject : Shoulder insignia. 1. It has been ascertained that the circular reestablishing shoulder insignia is not thoroughly understood. A great many interpret it as authorizing them to wear the insignia of the division, etc., in which they served in France; as a result insignia of demobilized divisions can be seen every day on the streets of Washington. 2. The fact that while <u>mandatory</u> on the seven regular divisions these insignia are merely <u>authorized</u> for the different services has escaped general observation. 3. A number of units wore insignia in France which were never approved by G.H.Q. For this reason it is deemed wise to publish a list of approved insignia applicable at this time."

In response, on 10 June 1920 WAR DEPARTMENT issued:

"Circular No. 214. SHOULDER PATCH INSIGNIA — INTERPRETATION OF CIRCULAR NO. 164, WAR DEPARTMENT, 1920. 1. The provisions of Circular No.164, War Department, 1920 (Shoulder Patch Insignia), appear to be largely misunderstood. That circular reestablishes the shoulder patch insignia approved by General Headquarters, American Expeditionary Forces, in France, for such organizations as are now in existence in the Army, and applies to present and future members of such organizations. It does not authorize individuals now in the service to wear the insignia of the organization to which they belonged during The World War unless they are at present members of the organization. 2. The circular is mandatory for the seven Regular Army divisions. Insignia of staff corps, departments and operating services are permitted when authorized by the chief of the respective staff corps, department or operating service. 3. The following insignia are authorized under the foregoing without further reference to the War Department:

Approved by G.H.Q., A.E.F.

G.H.Q.., A.E.F.	5th Division
1st Division	6th Division
2nd Division	7th Division
3rd Division	Tank Corps
4th Division	Chemical Warfare Service

Approved by War Department

    Overseas Couriers

    1st Gas Regiment, C.W.S.

    30th Artillery Brigade, C.A.C.

    31st Artillery Brigade, C.A.C.

4. No insignia other than those prescribed in paragraph 3 are authorized without approval of the War Department, except in the case of officers and enlisted men who are still retained in hospitals pending discharge for wounds or other disabilities incurred overseas. (421.7, A.G.O.)

By order of the Secretary of War."

On 6 September 1921, WAR DEPARTMENT issued:

"Circular No. 232. SHOULDER SLEEVE INSIGNIA – RESCISSION OF CIRCULARS NOS. 164 and 214, WAR DEPARTMENT, 1920.

Pending the publication of the revision of Uniform Regulations and Uniform Specifications, the following is published for the information and guidance of all concerned: 1. UNIFORM REGULATIONS. Insignia, shoulder sleeve.--Shoulder sleeve insignia of divisions, corps, armies, communications zone and headquarters of the field forces and the American Forces in Germany, will be worn by the personnel belonging to these organizations. Shoulder sleeve insignia will not be worn by any other organizations. It will be worn on the upper part of the left sleeve of the service coat or overcoat, the top of the insignia to be one-half inch below the top of the seam joining the sleeve to the coat or overcoat. 2. UNIFORM SPECIFICATIONS. Insignia, shoulder sleeve.--As per pattern approved by American Expeditionary Forces for those organizations (or their successors) which served in France in The World War. Divisions now organized or which may be organized in the future and which have not adopted shoulder sleeve insignia will send a design of the insignia which they desire to adopt for approval by the War Department. These insignia will be simple in design. 3. Circular No. 164, War Department, 1920 (Shoulder patch insignia), and Circular No. 214, War Department, 1920 (Shoulder patch insignia— Interpretation of Circular No. 164, War Department, 1920), are rescinded. (421.7, A.G.O.)

By order of the Secretary of War:"

**Approval Dates of Authorized Shoulder Sleeve Insignia
of the American Expeditionary Forces**

Unit	Date Distinctive Insignia Approved
G.H.Q., A.E.F.	7 February 1919
Armies	
First	16 November 1918
Second	11 December 1918
Third	30 January 1919
Corps	
I	3 December 1918
II	13 January 1919
III	3 December 1918 and 30 January 1919
IV	28 December 1918
V	3 December 1918
VI	1 January 1919
VII	19 November 1918
VIII	18 December 1918
IX	14 December 1918
Divisions	
1st	21 October 1918
2d	6 November 1918
3d	24 October 1918
4th	30 October 1918
5th	20 October 1918
6th	20 October 1918
7th	23 October 1918
8th	31 March 1919
26th	26 October 1918
27th	29 October 1918
28th	19 October 1918
29th	21 October 1918
30th	23 October 1918
31st	7 March 1919
32d	11 November 1918
33d	21 October 1918
34th	29 October 1918
35th	29 October 1918
36th	12 November 1918
37th	5 November 1918
38th	30 October 1918
39th	No design approved by G.H.Q., A.E.F.
40th	23 November 1918
41st	28 December 1918
42d	29 October 1918
76th	14 March 1919

77th	23 October 1918
78th	20 October 1918, 24 January 1919 and 8 March 1919
79th	16 November 1918
80th	20 October 1918
81st	19 October 1918
82d	21 October 1918 and 21 February 1919
83d	26 December 1918
84th	? Date not verified
85th	24 December 1918
86th	26 November 1918
87th	9 November 1918
88th	21 October 1918 and 12 November 1918
89th	25 October 1918
90th	25 October 1918
91st	8 December 1918
92d	20 October 1918 and 16 December 1918
93d	30 December 1918

Service and Other Units

Services of Supply – Base Units	24 December 1918 and 25 January 1919
Services of Supply – Advance Section	3 February 1919
Services of Supply – Intermediate Section, General Intermediate Storage Depot	11 June 1919
Regulating Stations and Railheads	16 January 1919
13th Engineers (Railway)	12 February 1919
Postal Express Service and Overseas Couriers	21 February 1919 and 5 May 1919
Central Records Office – Adjutant General's Department	27 January 1919
Ambulance Service	5 January 1919
Liaison Service	4 April 1919
Camp Pontanezen	7 May 1919
Chemical Warfare Service	18 January 1919
District of Paris	11 March 1919
North Russia Expeditionary Force	5 June 1919
Tank Corps	30 January 1919
Second Corps Schools	18 January 1919
Third Corps Schools	18 January 1919
Educational Corps – American E.F. University	18 April 1919
Fourth Marine Brigade	6 November 1918 (See 2nd Division)
Fifth Marine Brigade	20 June 1919

Approved Insignia of the American Expeditionary Forces

AMERICAN EXPEDITIONARY FORCES
DISTINCTIVE CLOTH INSIGNIA

ARMIES

CORPS

DIVISIONS

Charts of Approved Insignia of the American Expeditionary Forces. Printed at Base Printing Plant 29th Engineers U.S. Army 1919. (Based on the unit insignia depicted as approved, it is believed the charts were printed in February 1919 with the insignia approved through 7 February 1919. Believed to be the charts referred to in the 20 February 1919 response of Acting Chief, G-2-D. Pictured above is Armies, Corps and Divisions 1st – 6th).

Continued. Divisions 7th - 93rd.

AMERICAN EXPEDITIONARY FORCES
DISTINCTIVE CLOTH INSIGNIA

SHEET   NO.   2

G.H.Q.

CENTRAL
RECORDS OFFICE

REGULATING AND
RAILHEAD STATIONS

2ND CORPS SCHOOL

3RD CORPS SCHOOL

BASE SECTION S.O.S.

CHEMICAL WARFARE
SERVICE

U.S. AMBULANCE
SERVICE

TANK CORPS

ADVANCE SECTION S.O.S.

Sheet No. 2. G.H.Q., Other Services.

GENERAL HEADQUARTERS AMERICAN EXPEDITIONARY FORCES

SSI Approved: 7 February 1919
GENERAL HEADQUARTERS AMERICAN EXPEDITIONARY FORCES
"MEMORANDUM: No. 2   France, February 7, 1919.
1. The following arm insignia is approved and will be worn on the left arm of the service coats and outer garments, red stripe to be one inch from the shoulder seam, by all officers, field clerks and soldiers assigned to these Headquarters:

A disc of gros grain silk, 2 1/8 inches in diameter, with 3 horizontal stripes of red, white and blue of equal width at the perpendicular diameter of the disc; the disc to show through the hole of the same diameter cut in a circular piece of olive drab cloth 3 1/8 inches in diameter.

2. This arm insignia can be purchased at the clothing sales office of the Post Quartermaster and will be issued to soldiers at the rate of one arm insignia for each authorized garment described in paragraph 1 of this Bulletin.

By command of General Pershing:
Adjutant General."

Sample from the records of the National Archives.

Design painting from the records
of the National Archives.

General Headquarters
American Expeditionary Forces
Armies

FIRST ARMY
LINEAGE
    Organized 10 August 1918 in the Regular Army in France. Demobilized 20 April 1919 in France.
CAMPAIGN PARTICIPATION
    World War I
              St. Mihiel
              Meuse-Argonne
              Lorraine 1918
SSI Approved: 16 November 1918

    On 26 October 1918, Headquarters First Army issued GENERAL ORDERS, No. 28 wherein it stated "II. The following distinctive insignia has been adopted for Army Troops, First Army, to be worn on the left shoulder with top of the insignia at the shoulder seam of coat. A block "A" of black cloth as follows:" (See design below.) On 15 November 1918 Army Commander, First Army wrote Adjutant General, G.H.Q., American E.F. "1. It is requested that the distinctive insignia for Army Troops, First Army, and for the First, Third and Fifth Corps, as published in General Order No. 33, these Headquarters (copy herewith), be formally approved by and made of record at G.H.Q., American E.F." General Order No. 33 dated 9 November 1918 described the First Army insignia as "A Block Letter "A" of black cloth 4 inches long, 3 inches wide at top." On 16 November 1918 G.H.Q., A.E.F. by telegram to Commanding General, 1ˢᵗ Army advised "Number M-863. Reference section two General Orders twenty-eight Headquarters First Army comma design adopted as insignia for Army Troops First Army is approved period Submit by mail to this office sample or drawing with complete description thereof for records of these Headquarters." By 1ˢᵗ Ind. to the 15 November letter on 18 November G.H.Q., American E. F. to Commanding General, 1ˢᵗ Army advised "Approval has already been made of design selected for Army

Troops, 1ˢᵗ Army. With regard to insignia of 1ˢᵗ, 3d and 5ᵗʰ Corps, information is requested as to whether the wearing of said insignia is to be limited to Corps Troops. Upon receipt of the desired information, and of drawings of the designs selected, decision as to approval will be made. Attention is invited to the fact that approval of all distinctive designs for units of the A.E F. will be made at G.H.Q." (See First, Third, and Fifth Corps hereinafter.)

Symbolism: The "A" represents the first letter in the alphabet
                     and thus the unit's designation.

(Note: On 14 December 1918, by MEMORANDUM NO. 45, Headquarters First Army by Command of Lieutenant General Liggett approved a headquarters insignia with red in the upper portion and white in the lower portion of the block "A" and 14 other variations with color and symbolic additions to the lower segment of the "A" for the various services. Absent verification of G.H.Q., A.E.F. approval the variations are _not_ considered authorized SSI. In fact, G.H.Q., A.E.F. in Memorandum of 19 November 1919 notes that the insignia for First Army Headquarters was not approved.)

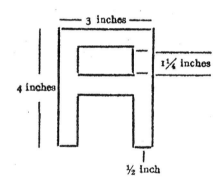

Design depicted in General Orders, No. 28, Headquarters First Army of 26 October 1918.

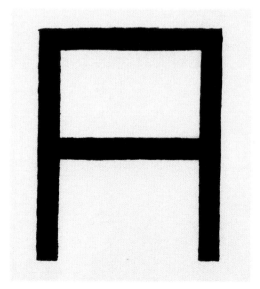

Design painting from the records
of the National Archives.

SECOND ARMY
LINEAGE
Organized 20 September 1918 in the Regular Army at Toul, Meurtheet-Moselle, France. Demobilized 15 April 1919 in France
CAMPAIGN PARTICIPATION
World War I
Lorraine 1918
SSI Approved: 11 December 1918

On 8 December 1918 Commanding General, Second Army, by letter to Adjutant General, G.H.Q., American E. F. wrote "1. Request that the attached design of Insignia to be worn by army troops of the Second Army be approved. Although telegram from G.H.Q., American E.F., dated October 18th, 1918, referred to divisions, it is understood that the First and Third Armies have adopted an insignia for army troops." A design was attached depicting a block numeral 2 with red on the top half and white on the bottom half. The corners of the upper red portion are clipped. By telegram on 11 December 1918 from G.H.Q., A.E.F. to Commanding General, 2nd Army advised "M-1012 Distinctive design as submitted by your letter December eighth approved for army troops second army period."

Symbolism: Red and white are the colors associated with armies, while the numeral "2" identifies the unit's designation.

Design accompanying 8 December 1918 letter of Commanding General, Second Division to Adjutant General, G.H.Q., American. E.F.

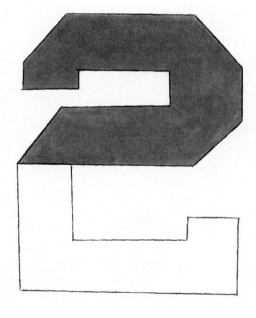

Design painting from the records of the National Archives.

THIRD ARMY
LINEAGE
Established 7 November 1918 and organized 7-15 November 1918 in the Regular Army at Ligny-en-Barrois, France, as Headquarters and Headquarters Troop, Third Army. Demobilized 2 July 1919 in Germany. Staff became American Forces Germany.
CAMPAIGN PARTICIPATION
World War I
None
SSI Approved: 30 January 1919 (after resubmission)

On 12 December 1918 Adjutant General, G.H.Q., A.E.F. by telegram to Commanding General, 3rd Army wrote "M-1019 Submit by mail to this office for approval sample or drawing with complete description thereof of insignia desired for Army Troops Third Army period This design is to be worn by every officer and man of the Army Troops comma Third Army period If design submitted is approved report will be made by telegram from this office." On 15 December 1918 Commanding General, 3d Army, Am.E.F. by letter to Adjutant General, G.H.Q., Am.E.F. wrote "1. Enclosed is a sample of the insignia desired officially approved for wear by 3d Army troops. 2. This sample was made locally and is not symmetrical but gives a very correct idea of what is desired. 3. Size and dimensions are approximately correct." By 1st Ind. on 18 December 1918 the Adjutant General, G.H.Q., American E. F. to Commanding General, 3d Army wrote "Owing to the fact that approved distinctive insignia for the 1st Army is the letter "A", the enclosed proposed insignia for the 3d Army cannot be approved. New design will be submitted with least practicable delay." On 20 December 1918 by 2nd Ind. Hq. Third Army, American E.F. To Adjutant General, G.H.Q., American E.F. wrote "1. Requesting reconsideration, and inviting attention to attached insignia of First and Third Armies, from which it will be seen that the design for Third Army in no way resembles that of the First Army, and in addition some 15,000 of the proposed designs for the Third Army have been issued and are now being worn by officers and enlisted men of Army Headquarters and Army troops." In reply on 20 December 1918 by telegram from HAEF to "COMMANDING GEN THIRD ARMY COBLENZ NUMBER 1078 PERIOD CONFIRMING TELEPHONE CONVERSATION THIS AFTERNOON WITH GENERAL CRAIG COMMA THE DISTINCTIVE INSIGNIA FOR THE THIRD ARMY IS APPROVED". On 28 December Adjutant General, HAEF wrote C G 3RD ARMY "M-1043 SEND SAMPLE OR DRAWING OF APPROVED INSIGNIA FOR THIRD ARMY TO THESE HEADQUARTERS WITH LEAST POSSIBLE DELAY AS SAME HAS NOT BEEN RECEIVED". On same date Hq. Third Army by a 1st Ind. to Adjutant General, G.H.Q., American E.F. wrote "1. Inclosed herewith is drawing of Third Army insignia as called for in above telegram." The drawing shown below was inclosed. Subsequently, on 30 January 1919 by a 2nd Ind. G. Hq., A. E. F. to Commanding General, 3rd Army wrote "Approved." The insignia is described as follows: on a blue disc 2 1/4 inches in diameter a white letter "A" within a red circle with an outer diameter of 2 inches and an inner diameter of 1 5/8 inches. Elements of the "A" 1/8 inch.

Symbolism: The disc with two borders alludes to the designation of the unit, and the letter "A" signifies "army." The "A" inside an "O" also stands for the Army of Occupation and the red, white, and blue national colors.

Drawing accompanying 28 December 1918 1st Ind. from Headquarters Third Army to Adjutant General, G.H.Q., American E.F.

Design painting from the records of the National Archives.

Corps

FIRST ARMY CORPS (I Corps)
LINEAGE
   Organized 15-20 January 1918 in the Regular Army at Neufchateau, France, as Headquarters, I Army Corps. Demobilized 25 March 1919 in France
CAMPAIGN PARTICIPATION
   World War I
      Champagne-Marne
      Aisne-Marne
      St. Mihiel
      Meuse-Argonne
      Ile de France 1918
      Champagne 1918
      Lorraine 1918
SSI Approved: 3 December 1918

   On 20 October 1918 HEADQUARTERS FIRST ARMY OFFICE CHIEF OF STAFF wrote Commanding Generals, 1st, 3rd and 5th Corps "SUBJECT: Insignia for Corps Troops. 1. The matter of the wearing of special insignia to distinguish the various divisions has been taken up. It is desired to extend this to include Corps troops. 2. You are therefore requested to submit a design for a cloth badge to be worn on the left shoulder for the Corps Troops of your Corps. The pattern should be the same for all Corps Troops, and should have different initials or some other feature upon it, to distinguish men belonging to Corps Artillery, Signal Troops, etc., etc." On 23 October 1918 Hq., 1st Army Corps replied by 1st Ind. "1. The 1st Corps had already adopted as its Corps insignia a circle. 2. To carry out the color scheme the circle should in all cases be white and the distinguishing marks inside the circle dark blue except as noted below. 3. As appropriate distinguishing marks the following are desired for adoption (all marks being within the circle):" 20 distinguishing marks were listed. The 1ˢᵗ Ind. continued "4. The above distinguishing marks might be used for the Corps troops of any Corps whatever, provided they could fit them to their Corps insignia. 5. While a simple circle would suffice for all Corps troops it is believed that the idea is to distinguish each separate element and thereby contribute to espirit and morale." On 28 October Headquarters First Army by 2ⁿᵈ Ind. advised Commanding General, I Corps "1. The adoption of a circle as the distinctive design for the I Corps is approved. Approval of the recommendation for other distinguishing marks is suspended as it is desired to obtain at once a means of distinguishing Corps troops as such. 2. A requisition for the circle design for all Corps troops to be worn on the left shoulder will be submitted at once. 3. This paper to be returned." Subsequently, on 7 November 1918 Commanding General, 1ˢᵗ Army advised Commanding General, 1ˢᵗ, 3ʳᵈ, 5ᵗʰ Corps "1. You have already been informed of the approved shoulder insignia for the troops of your Corps. 2. The Chief Quartermaster, 1ˢᵗ Army, has taken the following steps to procure these insignia: He has arranged with the Purchasing Agent in Paris to procure the insignia, which will be made up and furnished the troops upon requisition. If this requisition has not already been submitted it should be submitted without delay. The length of time necessary for the delivery of these insignia is problematical. 3. It is most desirable that these insignia should be placed on the men with the least practicable delay. In order to anticipate the deliveries on requisition above referred to, it is desired that each Corps Commander take steps to have the various organizations provide themselves at once with the insignia wherever it is possible. As the cloth of the prescribed color will probably not be readily available, the temporary expedient may be adopted of using khaki or olive drab cloth or some other colored cloth cut according to a pattern which can be furnished by the Corps Headquarters to the organizations. The different authorized designs vary sufficiently in shape to permit the classification of a man as to his Division or Corps in that way irrespective of the color of the insignia. …" (This explains why some insignia herein referenced may have a background of khaki or olive drab instead of the prescribed color.) General Orders No. 33 of First Army dated 9 November listed the I Corps insignia as "White circle on dark blue background." On 15 November 1918 Army Commander, First Army to Adjutant General, G.H.Q., American E.F. wrote: "1. It is requested that the distinctive insignia for Army Troops, First Army, and for the First, Third and Fifth Corps, as published in General Order No.33, these Headquarters (copy herewith), be formally approved by and made of record at G.H.Q. American E.F." By 1ˢᵗ Ind. of 18 November 1918 G.H.Q., American E.F. replied to Commanding General, 1ˢᵗ Army "Approval has already been made of design selected for Army Troops, 1ˢᵗ Army. With regard to insignia of 1ˢᵗ, 3ʳᵈ and 5ᵗʰ Corps, information is requested as to whether the wearing of said insignia is to be limited to Corps Troops. Upon receipt of the desired information and of drawings of designs selected, decision as to approval will be made. Attention is invited to the fact that approval of all distinctive designs for units of the A.E.F. will be made at G.H.Q." On 1 December 1918 Headquarters, First Army by 2d Ind. to C in C General Headquarters, American E.F. wrote "1. Returned. Drawings of designs selected for the distinguishing insignias of the I, III and V Corps herewith. The wearing of these insignias is to be limited to Corps Troops concerned." The drawings of the three Corps insignia as provided by First Army, Office of Chief Quartermaster - Supply Division were attached. The I Corps design was a "White circle on olive drab back ground" with an inner diameter of 6cm and greater diameter of 8cm. On 3 December 1918 G.H.Q., A.E.F.

by telegram to Cmdg General First Army "M-960 Distinctive designs submitted for Corps troops of First comma third and fifth corps are approved." A subsequent description by I Corps to Adjutant General, G.H.Q., A.E.F. on 25 February 1919 was "A white circle on dark blue square patch, dimensions – inside of circle four centimeters, outside of circle five and one half centimeters, size of patch seven centimeters." Thus, there is some question on background and size, although the approval reference to General Order 33 of First Army dated 9 November 1918 would verify the description as "White circle on dark blue back ground."

Symbolism: The circle or sphere alludes to the I Corps insignia of the Army of the Potomac from the Civil War and the white and blue the colors of corps distinguishing flags.

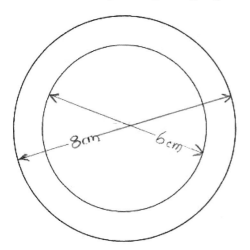
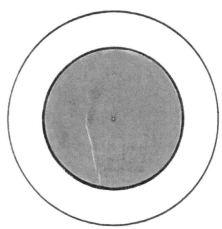

Drawing of design selected for I Corps sent by Chief of Staff, First Army on I December 1918 to C in C General Headquarters, American E.F. Note: Based on sample on file at Chief Quartermaster, First Army. Apparently on olive drab cloth in place of dark blue background as per First Army, General Orders No. 33 of 9 November 1918. Described as "White circle on olive drab back ground
Greater diameter   8 centimeters.
Inner   "   6   " ."

Design painting with white circle on an olive drab or khaki disc from the records of the National Archives.

Sample of white circle on blue background from the records of the National Archives.

SECOND ARMY CORPS (II Corps)
LINEAGE
    Organized 24 February 1918 in the Regular Army at Montreuil, France, as Headquarters II Army Corps. Demobilized 1 February 1919 in France.
CAMPAIGN PARTICIPATION
    World War I:
        Somme Offensive
SSI Approved: 13 January 1919

On 7 December 1918 by telegram from 2ND CORPS to C IN C HAEF wrote "416 G 1 PERIOD RE TEL M 674 OF OCTOBER 19TH IN REGARD TO DIVISIONAL INSIGNIA AUTHORIZED FOR CORPS TROOPS PERIOD INSIGNIA ADOPTED FOR THIS COMMAND IS BLUES STAR ON WHITE FIELD WITH RED INDIAN HEAD IN CENTER". In reply, on 8 December G.H.Q., A.E.F. wrote "M-968 Reference your four sixteen G one insignia of star with Indianhead has been already approved for second division period Submit new design for approval". By telegram of 12 December G.H.Q., A.E.F. to Commanding General, 2nd Corps wrote "M-1020 Submit by mail to this office for approval sample or drawing with complete description thereof of insignia desired for Corps Troops 2nd Corps period This design is to be worn by every officer and man of the Corps Troops comma second Corps period If design submitted is approved report will be made by telegram from this office period". On 16 December 1918 Commanding General, Second Corps, submitted to C. in C., G.H.Q., American E.F. "1. Reference your telegram M1020, enclosed is drawing of insignia for Corps Troops of the Second Corps for which authorization is requested. 2. The following description of the standard design, dimensions being given to indicate the proportions of the figure: A circle in blue 11.5 cm. in diameter composed of a line 4 mm. in width, having inscribed therein a five-pointed star in blue. Points of the star extended to outer edge of this circle. Superimposed on star a circle in white 5 cm. in diameter bearing the device of an Indian head in profile, facing to right, red, with shadows cast in solid tone of blue. Indian head filling space within an average distance of 4 mm. from outer edge of white circle. 3. It is understood that a star and Indian head similar to this has been approved for the Second Division. It is further understood, however, that the design of the Second Division is quite different in general appearance and there is further distinction in that this is in the colors, blue and white. This design was adopted for the Corps last July before it was known just what requirements for official approval were necessary, and has since then been in use in the Corps signs and other markings, although troops have not been authorized to wear it pending the attaining of official approval. It is believed that if there is sufficient dis-similarity from the Second Division design to make it distinctive a certain amount of similarity would not be inappropriate inasmuch as the numbers of the two organizations are the same. 4. In view of all the above circumstances, it is earnestly requested that this design be authorized." By 1st Ind. of 21 December from GHQ, American E.F. to Commanding General II Corps advised "It is regretted that approval of this insignia cannot be given. New design will be submitted for approval with the least practicable delay." On 29 December 1918 Commanding General II Corps wrote to C. in C., G.H.Q., American E.F. "1. Referring to your telegram M 1020 and first indorsement (Misc.) 201.08 A107, dated December 21, enclosed is drawing of insignia for the Corps

Troops of the Second Army Corps, for which authorization is requested. 2. The following is a description of the design: A circle 2.5 inches in diameter divided into two parts by tangent semi-circles, the left part blue, charged with a flying American eagle over two stars, in white; the right part white, charged with a British lion facing to the left, in blue. 3. The intention of the design is to represent the American eagle and British lion, within a symbol of unity, as typified by the operations of this command with the British Army." On the letter is the notation "Disapproved … JMW" (Adjutant General). Another second design was submitted by courier, and by telegram of G.H.Q., A.E.F. on 13 January 1919 to A.C. of S G-1, 2nd Corps wrote "M-103. Second choice design submitted by officer-courier this date approved comma American eagle with Roman Two and British Lion period".

Symbolism: The Roman numeral two indicates the unit's designation, while the American Eagle and the British Lion show that the organization operated with the British. The white and blue are the colors of corps distinguishing flags.

Design submitted by Second Army Corps to G.H.Q., A.E.F. 13 January 1919 and approved by telegram M-103 of same date. (Note that although referred to as the second design in the approval, it was in fact the third design submitted.)

Design painting from the records of the National Archives.

THIRD ARMY CORPS (III Corps)
LINEAGE
    Organized 16 May 1918 in the Regular Army at Mussy-sur-Seine, France, as Headquarters and Headquarters Troop, III Army Corps. Demobilized 9 August 1919 at Camp Sherman, Ohio
CAMPAIGN PARTICIPATION
    World War I
        Aisne-Marne
        Oise-Aisne
        Meuse-Argonne
        Champagne 1918
        Lorraine 1918
SSI Approved: 3 December 1918 and 30 January 1919

    See I Corps comments. On 22 October 1918 Third Army Corps Commanding General wrote to Commanding General, 1st Army "1. In reply to your letter of October 20th, regarding insignia to be worn on the uniform of Corps Troops, it is proposed that the insignia for this Corps be a three-pointed star, to be made of light blue cloth. 2. There being so many odd units among Corps Troops, it is thought that to attempt to have additional insignia to distinguish the different branches of service would result in such a complicated thing that the supply would be too difficult to be practicable." In First Army General Orders No. 33 of 9 November 1918 the insignia was so described. On 1 December 1918 by 2d. Ind. of Headquarters, First Army to C in C General Headquarters, American E.F. wrote "1. Returned. Drawings of designs selected for the distinctive insignias of the I, III and V Corps herewith. The wearing of there insignias is to be limited to the Corps Troops concerned." The design for III Corps reflected an "Equilateral Triangle - Sides 2.30 Centimeters. 3 Isosceles Triangles – Base 2.30 Centimeters with Altitude of 4 Cm. – Color "Light Blue"." The drawing showed an inverted equilateral triangle in the middle but no color was noted. G.H.Q., A.E.F. approved the design by telegram of 3 December 1918 "M 960 Distinctive designs for Corps Troops of First comma Third and Fifth Corps are approved". On 21 January 1919 Commanding General, Third Army Corps to Commanding General, Third Army communicated "1. On October 22nd a communication was forwarded to the First Army recommending as insignia for this Corps a three-pointed star, to be made of light blue cloth. This insignia was approved by the Army and adopted by the Corps. 2. The original insignia desired by the Corps was a three-pointed star of light blue cloth as above with a white triangle in the center, but this white triangle was left off in the original recommendation because of the difficulty at that time of obtaining the proper material and the necessity for immediate action in order to comply with the wishes of First Army. 3. Now that conditions have improved and the facilities are greater, it is desired to alter the Corps' insignia to conform to the insignia which the Corps originally desired. It is, therefore, requested that authority be granted to modify the Third Corps insignia in accordance with the attached sketch." By 1st Ind. of 24 January 1919 from Hq. Third Army to Adjutant General, G.H.Q., American E.F. recommended approval, and by 2nd Ind. of G. Hq. A. E. F. of 30 January 1919 to Commanding General, 3rd Army was approved. The drawing submitted reflected "White- equilateral, side 2.3cm. Blue- isosceles, base 2.3cm.,h.4cm."

Symbolism: The three points of the caltrop indicate the numerical designation
of the unit, and the white and blue are the colors of
corps distinguishing flags.

Design submitted 15 November 1918 by Army Commander, First Army to Adjutant General, G.H.Q., American E.F. Described as "Equilateral Triangle - Sides 2.30 Centimeters. 3 Isosceles Triangles – Base 2.30 Centimeters with Altitude of 4 Cm. – Color "Light Blue"." Approved by telegram M-960 of 3 December 1918.

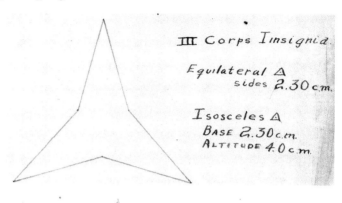

III Corps Insignia.

Equilateral △
sides 2.30 c.m.

Isosceles △
BASE 2.30 c.m.
ALTITUDE 4.0 c.m.

Design drawing attached to 21 January 1919 request for approval, and as approved 30 January 1919. Added provision for white triangle in center.

White~ equilateral, side 2.3 cm.
Blue ~ isosceles, base 2.3 cm., h.4 cm.

Design painting from the records of the National Archives.

FOURTH ARMY CORPS (IV Corps)
LINEAGE
   Organized 20 June 1918 in the Regular Army at Neufchateau, France, as Headquarters, IV Army Corps. Demobilized 11 May 1919 in Germany.
CAMPAIGN PARTICIPATION
   World War I
      St. Mihiel
      Lorraine 1918
SSI Approved: 28 December 1918

   On 12 December 1918 G.H.Q., A.E.F. by telegram to Commanding General, 4th Corps wrote "M-1021 Submit by mail to this office for approval sample or drawing with complete description thereof of insignia desired for Corps Troops fourth Corps period This design is to be worn by every officer and man of the Corps Troops comma fourth Corps period If design submitted is approved report will be made by telegram from this office period". On 15 December 1918 Commanding General, IV Army Corps, wrote Adjutant General, G.H.Q., American E.F. "1. Replying to your telegram of December 12th, there is inclosed herewith a sample of the device proposed for the Corps insignia, and a copy of the description thereof. 2. This device is the same device heretofore authorized for the insignia on the Corps automobiles." The description set forth by IV Corps on 15 December is as follows: "1. The distinctive cloth design for IV Corps is a circle divided into quadrants. The colors of the cloth in the quadrants are the Corps colors, namely blue and white, alternately arranged. The shade of blue is as per sample in the Office of the Corps Quartermaster. The diameter of the circle of the finished design is 1 ¾ inches. 2. This design will be worn on the left sleeve of all coats and overcoats of officers and enlisted men of the Corps Staff and Corps Troops. The device will be sewed on the sleeve one inch below the seam of the sleeve of the coat and placed so that the upper half circle will be white and blue, and the lower half circle, blue and white. ..." By 1st Ind. on 18 December G.H.Q., American E.F. advised "Owing to the fact that a design similar to attached has already been approved for a division, same cannot be approved for the IV Corps. A new design will be submitted without delay." By 2nd Ind. on 26 December Headquarters IV Army Corps wrote Adjutant General, G.H.Q., American E.F. "1. The design submitted December 15th, inclosed herewith and marked Sample 1, is one that was duly authorized for motor transportation of the IV Corps on September 21, 1918. (See copy of authority inclosed herewith). It has been in constant use by the Corps since that date and is not only well known throughout the Corps, but throughout the Third Army and the service in general. If the design "similar" to it already approved for a Division is not too much like this sample number one, it is recommended that the IV Corps be permitted to retain its design. (Sample No. 1.) 2. In case the above is not practicable, it is recommended that Sample No. 2, inclosed herewith, be approved as the design for IV Corps. A description of Sample 2 is inclosed herewith. 3. It is requested that decision in this matter be telegraphed." The following DESCRIPTION OF INSIGNIA FOR IV CORPS SLEEVE INSIGNIA (Sample No. 2) was attached "A square with sides 1 ¾ inches, divided into four triangular parts by the diagonals of the square. The triangles to be alternatively blue and white. The device to be sewed on the sleeve 1 ½ inches below the shoulder seam in such manner that the long dimensions of the blue triangles will be horizontal and the long dimensions of the white triangles vertical. Shades of color and methods of manufacture of design to be as per pattern in the office of the Corps Quartermaster." By telegram of 28 December 1918 from G.H.Q., American E.F. Commanding general, 4th Army Corps wrote "M-1145 Distinctive design number one as submitted by second indorsement dated December twenty sixth approved for fourth Army Corps period Matter of supply should be taken up with Chief Quartermaster period".

Symbolism: The disc divided into quadrants alludes to the numerical designation of the unit, and the white and blue are the colors of corps distinguishing flags.

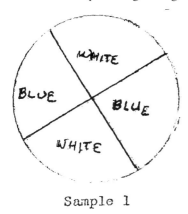

Sample 1

Design Sample 1 submitted to G.H.Q., American E.F. and approved 26 December 1918.

Above right: Copy of sample attached to 26 December 1918 communication of Headquarters Fourth Army Corps to G.H.Q., American E.F.

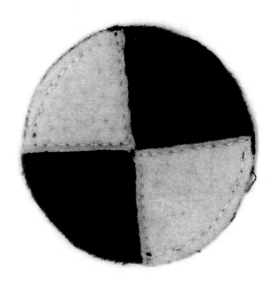

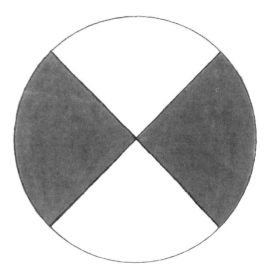

Design painting from the records of the National Archives.

FIFTH ARMY CORPS (V Corps)
LINEAGE
Organized 7-12 July 1918 in the Regular Army at Remiremont, France, as Headquarters and Headquarters Troop, V Army Corps. Demobilized 2 May 1919 at Camp Funston, Kansas.
CAMPAIGN PARTICIPATION
World War I
St. Mihiel
Meuse-Argonne
Lorraine 1918
SSI Approved: 3 December 1918

See I Corps comments. On 1 November 1918 Commanding General, 1st Army wrote Commanding General 5th Corps "1. No reply has yet been received to request from this office that you submit a suggested design for an insignia to be worn on left shoulder by Corps Troops. 2. These insignia are now being ordered and it is requested that you submit design for 5th Corps; least practicable delay." On 2 November V Corps replied by MEMORANDUM for Adjutant General, First Army "1. The accompanying sketch shows the approved insignia for Corps Troops, 5th Corps, - the insignia to be worn on left shoulder, point at shoulder seam. 2. It is requested that you notify the Chief Quartermaster to take steps immediately to provide these for the Corps Troops of this Corps." On 4 November HEADQUARTERS FIRST ARMY by MEMORANDUM To Chief Quartermaster, First Army advised "1. The accompanying sketch shows the approved insignia for Corps Troops of the V Army Corps; the insignia to be worn on the left shoulder, point at the shoulder seam. 2. The deputy Chief of Staff has directed that you take immediate steps to provide these insignia for the Corps Troops of the V Army Corps." Subsequently in First Army General Orders No. 33 of 9 November 1918 the insignia was described as "A Pentagon with cream colored spokes running from each corner to the center." The sketch accompanying the 1 December 1918 2nd Ind. of Headquarters, First Army, American E.F. to C in C General Headquarters, American E.F. shows "A Pentagon with cream colored sides and spokes running from each corner to the center. Olive Drab back ground. The above drawing shows the exact dimensions of the model insignia." By measurement that insignia was 6 cm per side and the cream spokes and border .6 cm. (Although the accompanying sketches on file of I and III Corps appear to be to scale the V Corps size is questionable. Note that it was purportedly copied from the sample on hand at First Army, Office of Chief Quartermaster – Supply Division. The accompanying sketch depicts the insignia as 3.4 cm per side and the spokes and border .5 cm. Those dimensions appear more likely. A 2d. Ind. of 1 December from Headquarters, First Army to C in C General Headquarters, American E.F. advised "1. Returned. Drawings of designs selected for the distinctive insignias of the I, III and V Corps herewith. The wearing of these insignias is to be limited to the Corps troops concerned." On 3 December 1918 G.H.Q., A.E.F. to Commanding General via telegram wrote "M960 Distinctive designs submitted for Corps Troops of First comma Third and Fifth Corps are approved".

Subsequently, on 12 January 1919 Headquarters Fifth Army Corps issued General Orders No. 1. as follows: "1. (a) Pursuant to G. O. 33, 1918, Headquarters First Army, American E.F., the shoulder insignia therein described, with the additions provided for in this order, will be worn by the officers and men of the Fifth Army Corps Headquarters and Troops pertaining to the Fifth Army Corps. (b) Description of insignia: An indigo blue pentagon, three and one-quarter centimeters in diameter, with white spokes one-third centimeter wide and white border one-half centimeter wide, to be worn firmly sewed on left sleeve of blouse and overcoat with upper point of pentagon on the shoulder seam and in the center of the sleeve. (c) The following variations in the color of the triangles of the pentagon are prescribed to identify the arm of service – General Officers: all triangles gold with gold piping around entire insignia. All Corps Staff Officers other than General Officers: insignia as described in Paragraph 1 (b), edged with gold piping. Officers of Corps Troops: as prescribed for enlisted men of their commands, edged with piping of arm of service. Enlisted men, except as otherwise specified in this order: the bottom triangle of pentagon to be the color of arm of service as prescribed in G. O. No. 149, 1918, GHQ., A.E.F.; in the case of two colors indicating arm of service the two triangles on the right and left of the bottom triangle will show the colors; insignia for enlisted men will not be edged with piping. All triangles of the pentagon will be red in the case of the Military Police Corps. 2. All concerned are directed to conform in the provisions of this order with the least practicable delay. Pending the procurement of the insignia conforming to the description given in this order, the temporary use of the insignia as issued by the Corps Quartermaster is authorized. (421.AGO.) By Command of Major General Summerall:" In G.H.Q. American Expeditionary Forces, General Orders No. 149 of 5 September 1918 noted above was listed the numerous color combinations for piping to be applied on officers' overseas caps.

On 19 February 1919 the Adjutant General wrote Commanding General, 5th Corps "The Commander-in-Chief directs the you furnish, with the least practicable delay, to the Commanding General, S.O.S. a sample of the distinctive insignia authorized for your command with complete description and dimensions." By 1st Ind. on 23 February Commanding General, Fifth Army Corps, replied to Commanding General, S.O.S. "1. Herewith furnished copy of General Orders No. 1. Fifth Army Corps, prescribing the shoulder insignia to be worn by officers and troops of this Corps. 2. There is enclosed a staff officer's shoulder insignia as prescribed in the orders. This insignia is of the same size and dimensions as that worn by all other officers and troops of this command, as prescribed in General Orders No. 1." No record was found that verified approval of G.H.Q., A.E.F. of the variations described in General Orders No. 1 of Fifth Corps and thus are not considered authorized. However, the blue pentagon with white border and spokes was adopted.

Symbolism: The pentagon represents the numerical designation of the unit, and the white and blue are the colors of corps distinguishing flags.

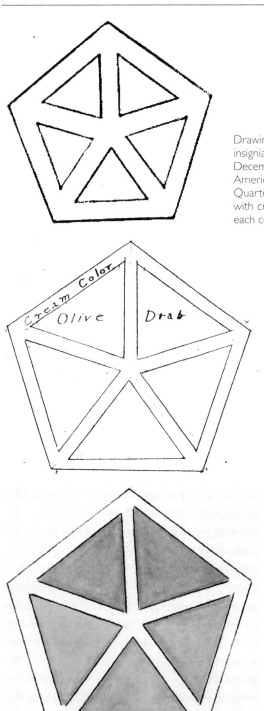

Drawing of design selected for V Corps distinctive insignia as sent by Chief of Staff, First Army on 1 December 1918 to C in C General Headquarters, American E.F. Note: Based on sample on file at Chief Quartermaster, First Army. Described as a Pentagon with cream colored sides and spokes running from each corner to the center. Olive drab background.

Drawing of design selected for V Corps distinctive insignia as sent by Chief of Staff, First Army on 1 December 1918 to C in C General Headquarters, American E.F. Based on sample on file at Chief Quartermaster, First Army. Approved by telegram M-960 of 3 December 1918.

Design painting with cream pentagon on olive drab or khaki background from the records of the National Archives.

Sample from the records
of the National Archives.

Sample from the collection of The Johnson Brothers.

SIXTH ARMY CORPS (VI Corps)
LINEAGE
   Organized 23 July – 1 August 1918 in the Regular Army at Neufchateau, France as Headquarters, VI Army Corps. Demobilized in May 1919 at Camp Devens, Massachusetts.
CAMPAIGN PARTICIPATION
   World War I
         Lorraine, 1918
SSI Approved: 1 January 1919

   On 28 December HQRS Sixth A C by telegram to Adjt. General GHQ. wrote "AG No two four seven period. Retel M six seven four period Sixth Army corps has adopted the following insignia colon Six pointed blue and white star upon white and blue background period. Approval requested." By telegram on 29 December G.H.Q., A.E.F. advised Commanding General, Sixth Corps by telegram "M-1149. Reference your telegram AG two four seven comma six pointed star has been authorized for insignia of Sixth Division period Submit new design for approval period". On 30 December by telegram from HQRS. SIXTH ARMY CORPS to ADJUTANT GENERAL G. HQ. wrote "AG TWO FIVE SIX PERIOD. RETEL M ONE ONE FOUR NINE SUBMIT WHITE STAR WITH SIX POINTS ON CIRCULAR BLUE BACK GROUND AS SIXTH CORPS INSIGNIA PERIOD. DOES NOT COLOR DISTINGUISH THIS FROM BLACK STAR OF SIXTH DIVISION PERIOD. SIMILAR STAR BELIEVED TO BE SIXTH CORPS INSIGNIA IN CIVIL WAR." In reply of 31 December G.H.Q., A.E.F. to Commanding General 6th Corps advised by telegram "M-1167. Reference your telegram AG-256 comma no more stars will be authorized as distinctive insignia period New design should be submitted promptly period". By telegram on 1 January 1919 Hqrs 6th army corps to Adjutant General G H Q wrote "AG two six one period insignia adopted by sixth corps colon white figure six on circular blue field comma approval recommended" By telegram of 1 January 1919 to Commanding General, 6th Army Corps, G.H.Q., A.E.F. replied "M-4 Reference your telegram A G two six one period Distinctive cloth insignia adopted by sixth Corps approved period Submit sample to this office without delay period Matter of supply should be taken up with Chief Quartermaster". On 2 January 1919 Commanding General, 6th Army Corps to Commander-in-Chief, G.H.Q., American E.F. wrote "1. In compliance with instructions contained in Telegram M-4, dated January 1, 1919, enclosed herewith sample of distinctive insignia adopted by 6th Army Corps and approved by G.H.Q."

Symbolism: The numeral "6" identifies the
                 corps' designation, while blue
                 and white are the colors of
                 corps distinguishing flags.

Drawing of design inclosed with 2 January 1919 communication of Commanding General, 6th Army Corps to Commander-in-Chief, G.H.Q., American E.F.

SEVENTH ARMY CORPS (VII Corps)
LINEAGE

Organized 19 August 1918 in the Regular Army at Remiremont, France, as Headquarters and Headquarters Troop, VII Army Corps. Demobilized 9-11 July 1919 at Camp Upton, New York.

CAMPAIGN PARTICIPATION
    World War I
        Streamer with inscription
SSI Approved: 19 November 1918

On 14 November 1918, Headquarters Seventh Army Corps to Commanding General, First Army wrote "1. In compliance with General Orders No. 33, First Army, the inclosed design of distinctive insignia for the Seventh Corps is submitted for approval." By 1st Ind. of 15 November Headquarters First Army to Commander-in-Chief, G.H.Q. American E.F. wrote "1. Recommending approval." The proposed design "White figure 7 on a shield of cobalt blue, to be sewed on a patch of khaki 5 ½ cm. sq." On 19 November 1918 Commander-in-Chief to Commanding General, 7th ARMY CORPS advised: "1. Reference your letter of November 14, 1918, addressed to Commanding General, 1st Army, relative to Corps insignia, the design submitted is approved as the distinctive insignia for Seventh Corps."

Symbolism: The numeral "7" indicates the corps' numerical designation, and blue and white are corps colors.

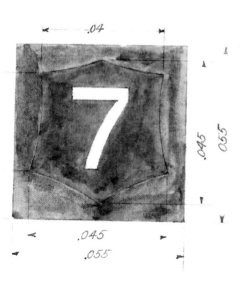

Design painting from the records of the National Archives.

Drawing of design for VII Corps distinctive insignia inclosed with communication of 14 November 1918 from Headquarters Seventh Army Corps to Commanding General, First Army. Described as: "White figure 7 on a shield of cobalt blue, to be sewed on a patch of khaki 5 ½ cm. sq."

EIGHTH ARMY CORPS (VIII Corps)
LINEAGE
Organized 26-29 November 1918 in the Regular Army at Montigny-sur-Aube, France. Demobilized 20 April 1919 in France.
CAMPAIGN PARTICIPATION
World War I
None
SSI Approved: 18 December 1918

On 12 December 1918 G.H.Q., A.E.F. advised Commanding General, 8th Corps by telegram "M-1022 submit by mail to this office for approval sample or drawing with complete description thereof insignia desired for Corps Troops eighth Corps period This design is to be worn by every officer and man of the Corps Troops comma eighth Corps period If design submitted is approved report will be made by telegram from this office period". On 16 December 1918 Corps Commander, Eighth Army Corps wrote to Adjutant General, G. H. Q. American E. F. "1. In compliance with your M-1022, December 12, inclosed design of insignia for 8th Corps Troops is submitted for approval." On 18 December G.H.Q., A.E.F. replied to Commanding General, 8th Corps by telegram "M-1051 Distinctive design submitted by your letter December sixteenth approved for corps troops eighth Corps period Matter of supply of insignia should be taken up with Chief Quartermaster period" The design a white block numeral 8 on a blue octagon. By a 1st Ind. of Feb. 21,1919 Commanding General, 8th Army Corps, wrote to Commanding General, S.O.S. "1. Inclosing sample of distinctive insignia for 8th Army Corps with description and dimensions, as directed herein." "Insignia for Enlisted men. 8th Corps. Description of VIII Corps Distinctive Mark: Insignia to be octagonal in shape and is composed of a blue field, blue as in the U.S. Flag, bearing a white eight and a white border around the edge, to conform with the following specifications: The maximum diameter of the insignia to be 2 inches, the white border around the edge to be 1/16 inch wide. The eight is to be octagonal in shape and is to be centered with the sides parallel to the sides of the sides of the insignia, the maximum diameter of the bottom part of the eight to be 7/8 inches, the maximum diameter of the top of the eight is to be 3/4 inches. The line forming the eight is to be 1/8 inch wide. Material: Any suitable, non-shrinkable cloth of fast color. Insignia for Officers. 8th Corps. Description: Same as for enlisted men except that the border and figure are embroidered in silver material. Distinctive design for eighth Corps approved telegram M-1051 HAEF, Dec.18, 1918."
No record found of the variation aforesaid to add a white border to the insignia as originally approved by G.H.Q., A.E.F. 18 December 1918.

Symbolism: The octagon represents the numerical designation of the unit, and
           the white and blue are the colors of corps distinguishing flags.

Drawing of design for VIII Corps insignia inclosed with communication of 16 December 1918 of Corps Commander, Eighth Army Corps to Adjutant General, G.H.Q., A.E.F. Described as: "A white block numeral 8 on a blue octagon."

Design painting from the records of the National Archives.

NINTH ARMY CORPS (IX Corps)
LINEAGE
    Organized 25-29 November 1918 in the Regular Army at Ligny-en-Barrois, France, as
Headquarters, IX Army Corps. Demobilized 5 May 1919 in France.
CAMPAIGN PARTICIPATION
    World War I
        None
SSI Approved: 14 December 1918

    On 1 December 1918 by telegram from Ninth Corps Commanding General to C.G.,
A.E.F. wrote "REQUEST APPROVAL OF THE FOLLOWING CORPS INSIGNIA
COLON: RED CIRCULAR BAND COMMA, THREE EIGHTS INCHES WIDE
COMMA, WITH OUTER DIAMETER TWO AND ONE HALF INCHES COMMA,
ENCLOSING IX OF LIKE DIMENSOINS ALL SUPERIMPOSED ON A PRUSSIAN
BLUE CIRCLE COMMA THREE INCHES IN DIAMETER PERIOD SAMPLE WILL
FOLLOW BY MAIL" On 11 December 1918 Commanding General, Ninth Corps wrote
to Commanding General, American Expeditionary Forces "1. Approval is requested of the
following Ninth Corps insignia: Red circular band 3/8 inch wide, with outer diameter of
2 1/2 inches, enclosing IX of like dimensions, all superimposed on a Prussian Blue circle,
three inches in diameter. 2. Sample herein enclosed." By 1st Ind. of 14 December 1918 from
G.H.Q. American E.F. to the Commanding General, Ninth Corps "Returned. Approved."

Symbolism: The Roman numeral "IX" represents the numerical designation of the unit.

Design painting from the records of the National Archives.

Sample from the records of the National Archives.

Divisions

FIRST DIVISION
LINEAGE
   Constituted 24 May 1917 in the Regular Army as Headquarters, 1st Expeditionary Division. Organized 8 June 1917 at New York, New York. Redesignated 6 July 1917 as Headquarters, 1st Division.
CAMPAIGN PARTICIPATION
World War I
         Montdidier-Noyon
         Aisne-Marne
         St. Mihiel
         Meuse-Argonne
         Lorraine 1917
         Lorraine 1918
         Picardy 1918
SSI Approved: 21 October 1918 and as revised 30 November 1918

   On 20 October HEADQUARTERS 1st DIVISION by telegram to C G HAEF wrote "G ONE FIVE SEVEN FOUR A PERIOD REFERENCE YOUR TELEGRAM NUMBER M SIX SEVEN FOUR PERIOD DISTINCTIVE DESIGN ADOPTED FOR ANNA IS A RED FIGURE ONE ABOUT FIVE INCHES HIGH EXTENDING DOWN FROM SEAM ON LEFT SHOULDER" (ANNA code name for 1st Division). By telegram of 21 October G.H.Q., A.E.F. replied to Commanding General, 1st Division "Number M-696. Reference your telegram G one number five seven four comma design adopted by 1st Division is approved period submit by mail sample of design or drawing and complete description thereof for records of these Headquarters." Subsequently on 24 October G.H.Q., A.E.F. issued a memorandum with a list of the 16 Divisions that had submitted descriptions of distinctive designs and which had been approved, including the 1ˢᵗ Division as "Red figure "1" about 5 inches high."

On 28 October 1918 Commanding General, 1ˢᵗ Division wrote to Commanding General, American E. F. "1. In compliance with your telegram No. M 696 the accompanying drawing and description are submitted. 2. The insignia consists of an oblong chevron of O. D. cloth, approximately 2 ¼ inches wide by 3 ¾ inches long overall, which is cut away at the lower end to form a point whose sides enclose an angle of 90 degrees. Upon the chevron and in the center, is imposed a figure "1", 1 ¾ inches high, made of crimson cloth. 3. The chevron is to be worn at the top of the left sleeve, facing toward the front and set vertically, the top of the chevron being so placed that the upper corner touches the seam where the sleeve joins the shoulder, at about one-third the distance from the top of the shoulder to the center of the arm-pit." On 4 November First Army communicated that "3. … it is desired that each division and Corps Commander take steps to have the various organizations provide themselves at once with the insignia wherever it is possible. As the cloth of the prescribed color will probably not be readily available, the temporary expedient may be adopted of using khaki or olive-drab cloth or some other colored cloth cut according to a pattern which can be furnished by the Corps or Division Hq. to the organizations. The different authorized designs vary sufficiently in shape to permit the classification of a man as to his Division or Corps in a way irrespective of the color of the insignia. 4. The main point is to get a distinguishing mark on the men's arms at once, in order that the identification of stragglers and soldiers who are arrested for other causes may be facilitated. 5. With this end in view all men and officers pertaining to your division will have the authorized insignia of the proper shape, and of as uniform in color as possible, on their uniform by November 20ᵗʰ. After that date men found without it will be arrested as stragglers unless they are in detachments under control of a responsible officer." Much to the dismay of 1ˢᵗ Division it was found that an order to First Army, Supplies for 100,000 insignia on 26 October and acknowledged as received on the 27ᵗʰ· had been misplaced.

By Memorandum No. 15 on 23 November 1918 Headquarters First Division wrote To All Organizations: "1. The attached design shows the dimensions of the Division Insignia. The background is of O. D. Cloth and the letter is of Red cloth. 2. The Quartermaster is furnishing the red cloth for this insignia. The O. D. Cloth will not be furnished at the present time. 3. The pattern will be made and put on the coats and overcoats immediately." Then on 26 November 1918 Commanding General, 1ˢᵗ Division to Commanding General, First Army wrote: "1. It is requested that General Orders No. 33, Headquarters 1ˢᵗ Army, dated November 9ᵗʰ 1918, be amended insofar as they pertain to the Division insignia for the First Division. 2. The insignia consists of an oblong chevron of O. D. cloth 2 ½ inches wide by 3 ¾ inches long over all, which is cut away at the lower end to form a point whose sides inclose an angle of 90 degrees. Upon the chevron and in the center is inclosed a figure one 1 ¾ inches high made of crimson cloth. 3. The chevron is to be worn at the top of the left sleeve set vertically. Top of chevron to be so placed that the upper edge touches seam where the sleeve joins the shoulder. 4. A design of the insignia is attached hereto." By 1ˢᵗ Ind. on 2 Dec. 1918 Hq. 1ˢᵗ Army to C-in-C., G.H.Q., American E. F. wrote "1. Forwarded for action on design submitted. 2. Proper record of application for change in design has been made in connection with G.O. 33 these Hq. 3. 1ˢᵗ Division is no longer in this command." Also on 26 Nov. 1918 C.G., First Division wrote Commander in Chief, A.E.F., (Thru Military channels) attention A.G. "I, Reference to Paragraph 3, letter dated 28 October 1918 from Headquarters 1st Division, subject, "Sleeve Insignia for First Division". It is desired to alter the provisions of Paragraph 3 of this letter to read as follows: "Chevron is to be worn at top of the left sleeve set vertically. Top of chevron to be so place that the upper edge touches the seam where the seam joins the shoulder"." There is some confusion in the approval process in that while this communication was sent through Hq. First Army the 1st Division was being reassigned to Third Army, however, it appears the request was received at Hq. Third Army on 29 November and passed on by 1st Ind. to Commanding General, G. H. Q., American E. F., and received on 30 November 1918 and approved. In The LIST OF DIVISIONAL INSIGNIAS APPROVED BY GHQ TO DATE of 1 January 1919 by Office Chief Q.M. recites the description as revised aforesaid for the 1st Division. It is believed the initial approval date of Oct. 31,1918 on O.Q.M.G. sheet 5-2-6 is an error as the documents cited above verify the 21 October 1918 date.

Symbolism: The numeral "1" denotes the division's numerical designation.

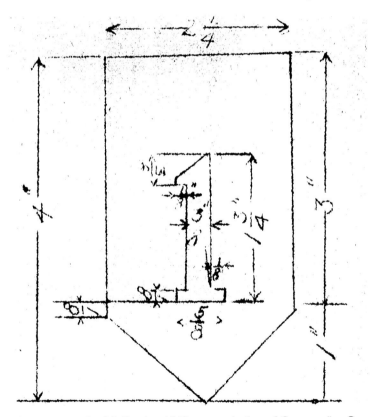

Drawing accompanying 28 October 1918 communication of Commanding General, 1st Division to Commanding General, American E.F. and Memorandum 15 of 23 November 1918. Note: Design is not consistent with initial 20 October 1918 description in telegram G 1 574 "RED FIGURE ONE ABOUT FIVE INCHES HIGH."

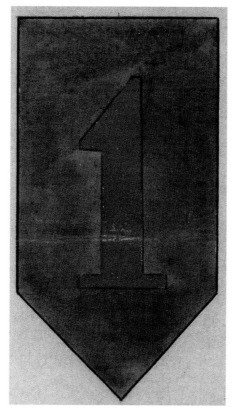

Design painting from the records of the National Archives.

Sample from the collection of the author depicting the design without the shield background.

SECOND DIVISION
LINEAGE
Constituted 21 September 1917 in Regular Army as Headquarters, 2d Division. Organized 26 October 1917 in France.
CAMPAIGN PARTICIPATION CREDIT
World War I
Aisne
Aisne-Marne
St. Mihiel
Meuse-Argonne
Ile de France 1918
Lorraine 1918
SSI Approved: 6 November 1918

On 20 October 1918 Commanding General, Second Division, Major General John A. Lejeune, U.S. Marine Corps, telegrammed C. G. HAEF "ATTENTION DE NUMBER TWO EIGHT TWO PERIOD REPLYING YOUR M SIX SEVEN FOUR SECOND DIVISION HAS CLOTH DESIGN CONSISTING OF RED AND BLUE INDIAN HEAD STAMPED ON WHITE CLOTH COMMA THE STAR SEWED ON CLOTH BACK GROUND COMMA THE SCHEME INVOLVES USING CLOTH BACK GROUND FOR STAR IN DIFFERENT COLORS AND SHAPES TO DESIGNATE DIFFERENT ORGANIZATIONS OF DIVISION COMMA STEPS HAVE ALREADY BEEN TAKEN TO PROCURE THIS DISTINCTIVE CLOTH DESIGN FOR THIS DIVISION PERIOD THE APPROVAL OF THE DESIGN IS REQUESTED" On 21 October G.H.Q., A.E.F. by telegram to Commanding General, 2d Division (and of 5th, 6th, 28th, 78th, 92d, and 80th Divisions) as follows: "Number M-704. Reference telegram relative Division insignia comma submit to this office by mail without delay sample of design adopted or drawing and complete description thereof for records of these Headquarters." Also on the 21st Commanding General,Second Division by letter to Commanding General, American E. F. wrote: "1. Referring to your telegram No. M-692 re division insignia, there is enclosed herewith on paper white star with Indian head stamped thereon. The proposed plan for design for this division involves the placing of the white star bearing the Indian head on cloth background, six (6) different colors of cloth to be used to designate different organizations. The enclosed sample of design may be considered merely as giving the idea. The Indian head to be used will be copied after the St. Gauden's head on the American gold five-dollar piece, which will be a considerable improvement over the enclosure. It is proposed to have the star made of heavy cloth. 2. The white star with the Indian head painted in two colors has been used in this division for some time and has already been painted on all transportation of the division. The design is already generally accepted as the division insignia, and prior to receipt of instructions from General Headquarters on the subject, steps had been taken to procure insignia of this design for issue to each officer and enlisted man in the division. The plans for procuring these designs are already underway, and it is urgently recommended that the design for insignia for the Second Division as submitted be approved and that approval be telegraphed at the earliest possible date, in order that there may be no delay in procuring and issuing the insignia. It is desired, if possible, to have the insignia issued before the division goes into the line again." G.H.Q., A.E.F. replied 6 November to Commanding General, 2d Division by telegram "Number M-809. Reference your letter of October twenty-first comma design submitted as insignia for Second Division is approved."

On 14 November 1918 Headquarters Second Division issued ORDERS No. 29:

"1. The following design of distinctive insignia, to be worn on the left shoulder with the top of the insignia at the shoulder seam of sleeve of coat, has been approved for Second Division troops to comply with paragraph 1. G. O. No. 33, Hq., 1ˢᵗ Army, A. E. F. and is published for the information of all concerned. 2. A five-pointed white star, having the head of an American Indian facing to the left, in red and blue, stamped or embroidered in center of star. The star will be of such dimensions as to be exactly contained in a circle of three and one-half (3 ½) inches in diameter. The star with Indian head will be superimposed on cloth backgrounds of various shapes and colors to designate the several organizations. 3. The cloth backgrounds will be of the following colors and shapes, the different shapes being of standard dimensions, in accordance with the accompanying drawings – particular attention being paid to accurately following these dimensions in order to insure the correct superimposing of the white star.

Div. Hdqrs.	Shield	Black cloth
3ʳᵈ Brig. Hdqrs.	Hexagon	" "
4ᵗʰ Brig. Hdqrs.	Oval (Horizontal)	" "
2ⁿᵈ F.A. Brig. Hq.	Oval (vertical)	" "
Hdqrs. troop	Shield	Yellow cloth
1ˢᵗ Fld. Sig. Bn.	Shield	Red cloth
Train Hq. & M.P.	Shield	Blue cloth
4ᵗʰ M. G. Bn.	Shield	Purple cloth
2ⁿᵈ Supply Train	Shield	Green cloth
2ⁿᵈ Amm. Train	Projectile	Green cloth
2ⁿᵈ Engr. Train	Castle	Green cloth
2ⁿᵈ Sanitary Tn.	Cross	Green cloth
5ᵗʰ M. G. Bn.	Hexagon	Purple cloth
6ᵗʰ M. G. Bn.	Oval (horizontal)	Purple cloth
2ⁿᵈ Trench Art.	Oval (vertical)	Purple cloth

9ᵗʰ Inf.	Pentagon	) Hq. and Hq. Co	Black cloth
23ʳᵈ Inf.	Circle	) Supply Co.	Green cloth
5ᵗʰ Marines	Square	) M. G. Co.	Purple cloth
6ᵗʰ "	Diamond	) 1ˢᵗ Battalion	Red cloth
12ᵗʰ F. A.	Oblong (horizontal)	) 2ⁿᵈ Battalion	Yellow cloth
15ᵗʰ F. A.	Oblong (vertical)	) 3ʳᵈ Battalion	Blue cloth
17ᵗʰ F. A.	Projectile	)	
2ⁿᵈ Engrs.	Castle	)	

4. Pending the receipt of the white star with the Indian head, organization commanders of this division will at once take the necessary steps to provide their troops with the cloth backgrounds as specified in this order."

Symbolism: The star and Indian head signify the American origins of the division.

Drawing of white star with Indian head design attached to 21 October 1918 communication of Commanding General, Second Division to Commanding General, American E.F. Note: Although this drawing is attached to the 21 October 1918 letter in the records of the National Archives, it is believed that this Indian head design is of greater detail than that originally attached and noted in the letter.

The following 13 drawings are representative of the 57 variations as set forth in Headquarters Second Division Orders No. 29 of 14 November 1918. From the records of the National Archives.

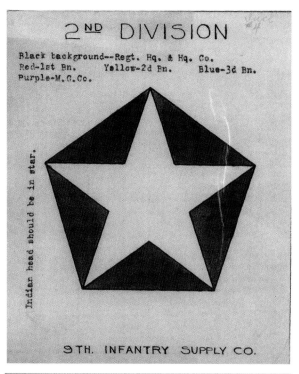

2ᴺᴰ DIVISION

Black background--Regt. Hq. & Hq. Co.
Red-1st Bn.   Yellow-2d Bn.   Blue-3d Bn.
Purple-M.G.Co.

Indian head should be in star.

9TH. INFANTRY SUPPLY CO.

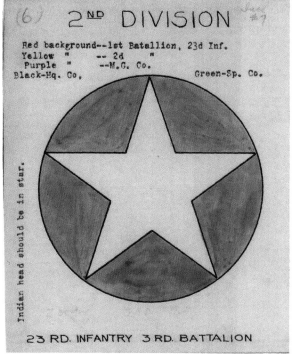

(6) 2ᴺᴰ DIVISION

Red background--1st Batallion, 23d Inf.
Yellow "   -- 2d   "
Purple "   --M.G. Co.
Black-Hq. Co,   Green-Sp. Co.

Indian head should be in star.

23 RD. INFANTRY 3 RD. BATTALION

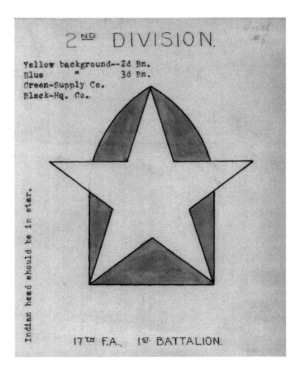

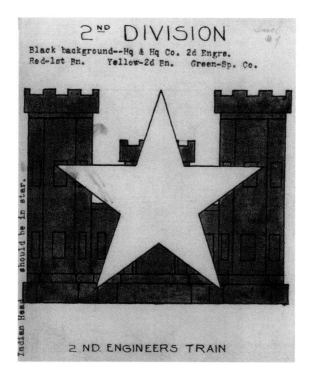

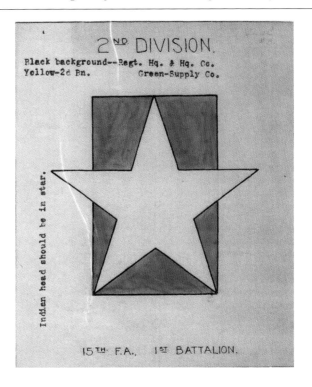

2 ND. DIVISION

Indian head should be in star.

2 ND. SANITARY TRAIN

2 ND. DIVISION

Red background--1st Bn.   Yellow-2d Bn.
Blue-3d Bn.   Black- Hq &Hq Co.
Green-Supply Co.

Indian head should be in star.

5TH. MARINES MACHINE GUN COMPANY

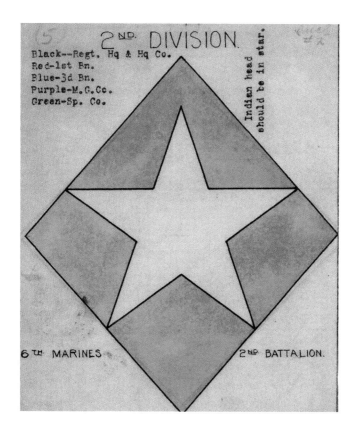

2 ND. DIVISION.

Black--Regt. Hq & Hq Co.
Red-1st Bn.
Blue-3d Bn.
Purple-M.G.Co.
Green-Sp. Co.

Indian head should be in star.

6 TH. MARINES   2 ND. BATTALION.

THIRD DIVISION
LINEAGE
Constituted 12 November 1917 in the Regular Army as Headquarters, 3d Division. Organized 21 November 1917 at Comp Greene, North Carolina.
CAMPAIGN PARTICIPATION
World War I
Aisne
Champagne-Marne
Aisne-Marne
St. Mihiel
Meuse-Argonne
Champagne 1918
Approved: 24 October 1918

On 23 October 1918 by telegram from Commanding General, 3rd Division to ADJUTANT GENERAL, AEF wrote "NUMBER THREE ONE SIX PERIOD IN COMPLIANCE YOUR TELEGRAM NUMBER M SIX SEVEN; FOUR FOLLOWING DESIGN ADOPTED FOR THIRD DIVISION PERIOD A PATCH OF ROYAL BLUE CLOTH TWO AND ONE QUARTER INCHES SQUARE HAVING DIAGONALLY ACROSS IT THREE WHITE STRIPES FIVE SIXTEENTH INCHES WIDE AND FIVE SIXTEENTH INCHES APART PERIOD DETAILED DIAGRAM FORWARDED BY MAIL PERIOD" By letter of the same date from Commanding General, 3rd Division to Adjutant General, American E. F. wrote "1. Confirming telegram No. 316, these headquarters, October 23, 1918, you will find inclosed diagram for insignia to be worn on the left sleeve of officers and enlisted men of the Third Division. 2. The color adopted for the ground is Royal Blue. The strips across the patch are to be white. 3. Immediately upon receipt of approval measures will be taken to have the insignia made." By telegram of 24 October 1918 G.H.Q., A.E.F. advised Commanding General, 3d Division.

"Number M-721. Reference your telegram Number three one six comma the design adopted by third division is approved."

Symbolism: The three white and three blue stripes are symbolic of six campaigns in which the division participated in WWI. The blue field symbolizes the loyalty of those who placed their lives on the altar of self-sacrifice in defense of the American ideals of liberty and democracy.

Drawing of design from the records of the National Archives.

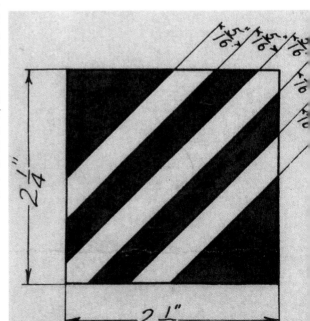

FOURTH DIVISION
LINEAGE

Constituted 19 November 1917 in the Regular Army as Headquarters, 4th Division. Organized 10 December 1917 at Comp Greene, North Carolina. Inactivated 21 September 1921 at Camp Lewis, Washington.

CAMPAIGN PARTICIPATION

World War I

   Aisne-Marne
   St. Mihiel
   Meuse-Argonne
   Champagne 1918
   Lorraine 1918

Approved: 30 October 1918

On 22 October 1918 a telegram was sent to ADJT GEN, GHQ AEF "NUMBER 1528 G 1 PERIOD FOLLOWING TELEGRAM RECD FROM IRENE REPEATED FOR YOUR INFORMATION QUOTE ADJT GENERAL AEF NUMBER FOUR FOUR NAUGHT REFERENCE YOUR M SIX SEVEN FOUR PERIOD FOURTH DIVN DESIGN ADOPTED UPON ORGANIZATION IS MADE UP OF FOUR IVY LEAVES PLACED IN CROSS SHAPE ABOUT SMALL CIRCLE PERIOD IF FOUND IMPRACTICABLE TO USE THIS DESIGN IN CLOTH UPON SLEEVE ON COAT ADJUST TO A SINGLE IVY LEAF WILL BE USED SIGNED CAMERON UNQUOTE" (Irene was code name for 4th Division.)By telegram of same date G.H.Q., A.E.F. advised Commanding General, 4th Division. "Number M-706. Reference your telegram Number four four naught comma submit by mail sample of drawing of design selected period Upon receipt of this comma decision as to approval will be made." By letter of 27 October 1918 Commanding General, 4th Division wrote The Adjutant General, H.A.E.F. "1 Reference your telegram # M-706, I am forwarding herewith for approval a drawing of the design selected for this division. 2. This is a divisional symbol which has been in use since the division was organized in December, of last year. If it is found practicable to have the entire symbol made in cloth, it is desired to do so. If it is not found practicable, I suggest one leaf from this design, stem downward." By telegram of 30 October from G.H.Q., A.E.F. to Commanding General, 4th Division advised "Number M-763. Reference your letter of October twenty-seventh comma design with four ivy leaves adopted as insignia for Fourth Division is approved."

The description was "Four green ivy leaves issuing from a circle. The leaves arranged per cross and the tips resting in the circumference of an imaginary circle 2 1/2" in diameter."

Symbolism: The four leaves allude to the numerical designation of the division, while the word "Ivy" as pronounced suggests the characters used in the formation of the Roman numeral "IV." Ivy leaves are symbolic of fidelity and tenacity.

Drawing (reduced) forwarded with communication of 27 October 1918 of Commanding General, Fourth Division to the Adjutant General, H.A.E.F. and noted thereon as "To be forwarded to G.H.Q. for approval."

Design painting from the records of the National Archives.

FIFTH DIVISION
LINEAGE
   Constituted 17 November 1917 in the Regular Army as Headquarters, 5th Division. Organized 11 December 1917 at Camp Logan, Texas. Inactivated 4 October 1921 at Camp Jackson, South Carolina.
CAMPAIGN PARTICIPATION
   World War I
      St. Mihiel
      Meuse-Argonne
      Alsace 1918
      Lorraine 1918
Approved: 20 October 1918

   On 19-20 October 1918 HQRS FIFTH DIVN sent a telegram to ADJUTANT GENERAL GHQ AEF "RETEL NUMBER M 674 COMMA THE DESIGN FOR THE FIFTH DIVISION TO BE WORN ON THE LEFT UPPER ARM IS A RED DIAMOND PERIOD THIS DESIGN HAS BEEN WORN BY THIS DIVISION AS INDICATED FOR A PERIOD ABOUT A MONTH PERIOD IT APPEARS ON ALL TRANSPORTATION AND WAS ADOPTED SOON AFTER THIS DIVISION WAS ORGANIZED REQUEST THAT IF ANOTHER DIVN MAKES REQUEST FOR THIS DESIGN THAT FIFTH DIVN BE GIVEN PREFERENCE PERIOD" By telegram of 20 October 1918 G.H.Q., A.E.F. replied to Commanding General, Fifth Division "Reference your telegram of October nineteenth the design of red diamond adopted by Fifth Division is approved." On 23 October Commanding General, Fifth Division wrote Commanding General, G.H.Q., A.E.F. "1. In compliance with your telegram No. M704, relative to Division insignia, the following design has been adopted and is being worn on the left sleeve of each officer and man of the Fifth Division: (Design is depicted in color) This diamond is made out of red cloth three inches long and two inches wide and is sewed on the blouse the top of the diamond against the shoulder seam of the sleeve, opposite the center of the shoulder strap…"
   On 22 December 1918 Chief of Staff, 5th Division wrote to Chief, G-1-D American E.F. "1. The insignia of the 5th Division is a red diamond. A sketch is enclosed. 2. Before the Division started for overseas service, the insignia was selected and placed upon all baggage as a distinctive mark in order that it could be easily segregated from the baggage of troops of other divisions which might be on the same transport. 3. Originally the red diamond had a white 5 in the center. After arrival in France the insignia was adopted as a red diamond without the white 5. Pursuant to Administrative Memorandum of the Division No. 24, issued August 20, 1918, it was placed on all transportation of the Division. On the 23rd day of September, 1918, Administrative Memorandum No. 37 was issued requiring that the insignia be worn on the left shoulder of all enlisted men and officers of the Division. 4. No significant meaning is recalled other than that the red was selected as a complement to the then Commanding General whose branch of the service was the Artillery. The following explanations have been made, however, as to the meaning of the Red Diamond: "Diamond dye – it never runs." "The Red Diamond represents a well–known problem in bridge building: it is made up of two adjacent isosceles triangles which make for the greatest

strength." 5. The Divisions nickname is "Red Diamond". It is reported that the Division was latterly known among the Germans opposed to it as the "Red Tigers" and the "Red Devils"."

Symbolism: As stated above.

Design depicted on 23 October 1918 communication of Commanding General, Fifth Division to Commanding General, G.H.Q., A.E.F.

Drawing accompanying 22 October 1918 communication of Commanding General, Sixth Division to Adjutant General, General Headquarters, Am. E. F. Note: In some descriptions the blue numeral 6 is not mentioned.

SIXTH DIVISION
LINEAGE

Constituted 16 November 1917 in the Regular Army as Headquarters, 6th Division. Organized 26 November 1917 at Camp McClellan, Alabama. Inactivated 30 September 1921 at Camp Grant, Illinois.

CAMPAIGN PARTICIPATION

World War I

Meuse-Argonne

Alsace 1918

Approved: 20 October 1918

On 20 October 1918 Commanding General Sixth Division sent a telegram to ADJUTANT GENERAL, GHQ AEF "G-1-366 PERIOD RETEL NUMBER M-6 74 SIXTH DIVISION PROPOSES ADOPTING CLOTH DESIGN SIX POINTED STAR PERIOD REQUEST APPROVAL END." In reply by telegram the same date G.H.Q., A.E.F. to Commanding General, Sixth Division wrote "M-689 Reference your telegram G one dash three six six October twentieth the design of six pointed star adopted by the Sixth Division is approved." In follow up the Commanding General, Sixth Division wrote Adjutant General, General Headquarters, Am. E. F. on 22 October "1. Reference telegram No. M-704, your headquarters, relative to insignia for this division, the inclosed design is submitted. The star is to be red of the actual size of the inclosed design and is to have superimposed thereon a blue "6"."

On 24 October 1918 the memorandum from General Headquarters American Expeditionary Forces setting forth "...a list of the Divisions which have submitted descriptions of the distinctive insignia adopted, and which have been approved by this office,..." described the design as: "Six pointed star." On the "LIST OF DIVISIONAL INSIGNIAS APPROVED BY GHQ TO DATE" by Office Chief Q.M. AEF of Jan. 1, 1919 the description is "Six pointed star of red cloth, with blue figure "6" superimposed." By communication of 22 Feb. 1919 Commanding General, 6th Division to Commanding General, S.O.S. wrote "1 In compliance with instructions contained in letter from the Adjutant General, Am. E. F., dated Feb. 19, 1919, the following is furnished you as the description of the distinctive insignia to be worn by members of this Division: Red Six Pointed Star, two inches from tip to tip. 2. A sample of this insignia is inclosed herewith."

On 20 June 1922, a memorandum from War Department General Staff to the Adjutant General of the Army stated "The Secretary of War directs that the drawing herewith be sent to the Quartermaster General, together with a communication in substance as follows: The shoulder sleeve insignia of the 6th Division was approved by telegram of October 20, 1918 from the Adjutant General, A. E. F., to Commanding General, 6th Division. It is described as follows: A red six pointed star (double triangles) whose points lie on an imaginary circle 2-1/2" in diameter."

Symbolism: The six pointed star alludes to the designation of the division (*see at left*).

SEVENTH DIVISION
LINEAGE
Constituted 6 December 1917 in the Regular Army as Headquarters, 7th Division. Organized 1 January 1918 at Camp Wheeler, Georgia. Inactivated 22 September 1921 at Camp Meade, Maryland.
CAMPAIGN PARTICIPATION
World War I
Lorraine 1918
Approved: 23 October 1918

On 22 October 1918 Headquarters, 7th Division telegrammed General Headquarters, A.E.F. the following "Number one five four G one period reference your number M six seven four period following design submitted for approval period two black equilatoral triangles with a base of three centimeters superimposed upon a red circle with a diameter of six centimeters comma the base of one triangle is horizontal comma with the apexes of the base angles resting on the circumference of the circle comma the second triangle inverted with the base parallel to the base of the first period an imaginary line bisecting the bases of both triangles would pass through their apexes and make the vertical diameter of the circle period design being forwarded by courier." On 23 October G.H.Q., A.E.F. advised by telegram to Commanding General, 7th Division "Number M-718. Reference your telegram Number one five four G one comma design adopted by 7th Division is approved."

In MEMORANDUM No. 9 of Headquarters Seventh Division of 27 January 1920 the design was described as: "Two black equilateral triangles with a base of three centimeters (1.18 inches) superimposed upon a red circle with a diameter of six centimeters (2.36 inches); the base of one triangle is horizontal, with apexes of the base angle resting on the circumference of the circle; the second triangle inverted with the base parallel to the base of the first. An imaginary line bisecting the bases of both triangles would pass through their apexes and make the vertical diameter of the circle."

Symbolism: The outline of an hourglass alludes to the numerical designation of the division, showing two "7's," one inverted, one upright.

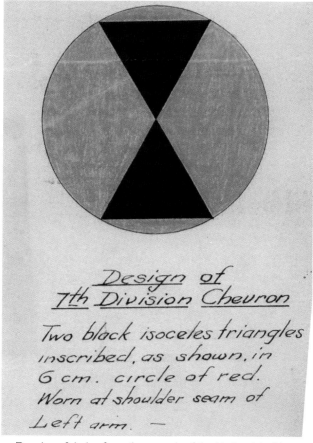

Drawing of design from the records of the National Archives.

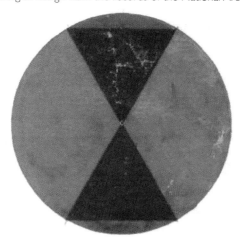

Design painting from the records
of the National Archives.

EIGHTH DIVISION
LINEAGE
Constituted 17 December 1917 in the Regular Army as Headquarters, 8th Division. Organized 5 January 1918 at Camp Freemont, California. Demobilized 5 September 1919 at Camp Lee, Virginia.
CAMPAIGN PARTICIPATION
World War I
Approved: 31 March 1919

On 22nd March, 1919, Headquarters, Eighth Division issued "GENERAL ORDERS No. 1) 1. Upon the approved findings of a Board of Officers appointed pursuant to Par. 1, Special Orders No. 7, Headquarters, Eighth Division, American Expeditionary Forces, 10th February 1919, the name "Pathfinder Division" is announced as the distinctive name of the Eighth Division. 2. The following Divisional Insignia has been adopted by the Eighth Division pursuant to the approved findings of a Board of Officers appointed pursuant to Par. 1, Special Orders No. 7, Headquarters, Eighth Division, American Expeditionary Forces, 10th February 1919: "A dark blue shield, with a silver figure "8", representing the Eighth Division, and a gold arrow, representing the "Pathfinder Division" imposed thereon; the arrow pointing perpendicularly upward thru the center of the figure "8", passing over the lower part, under the center part and over the upper part of the "8". " Subsequently on 22nd March 1919 The Commanding General, Eighth Division to The Commanding General, S.O.S. wrote: "1. Upon the approved findings of a Board of Officers appointed for the purpose, the Eighth Division has adopted the distinctive name of "Pathfinder Division", and a Divisional Insignia, described as follows: "A dark blue shield, with a silver figure "8", representing the Eighth Division, and a gold arrow, representing the "Pathfinder Division" imposed thereon; the arrow pointing perpendicular upward thru the center of the figure "8", passing over the lower part, under the center part and over the upper part of the "8". ". 2. A copy of the order announcing the Distinctive Name and Divisional Insignia is enclosed herewith, together with a model of the Insignia." By 1st Ind. of 31 March 1919 G.H.Q., American E.F. to Commanding General, Base Section #5 wrote "Approved, for so much of 8th Division only as is in France."

On 21 June 1922, a memorandum from War Department General Staff to the Adjutant General of the Army stated "The Secretary of War directs that the drawing herewith be sent to the Quartermaster General, together with a communication in substance as follows: The shoulder sleeve insignia of the 8th Division was approved by telegram of April 8, 1919 from the Adjutant General, A. E. F., to Commanding General, 8th Division. It is described as follows: "On a blue shield approximately 2 - 1/2" in height and 1 – 3/4" in width a yellow arrow pointed up 2 – 1/4" long surmounted by a white Arabic figure "8", 1 – 1/2" in height."

It is believed the 1st Ind. of 31 March 1919 from G.H.Q., A.E.F. to Commanding General Base Section #5 noted above is the correct approval date. The telegram 8 April 1919 referenced above was not found in the records reviewed.

Symbolism: The nickname of the division, "Pathfinder," is represented by the arrow, while the figure "8" identifies the numerical designation of the division.

Design painting from the records of the National Archives.

TWENTY-SIXTH DIVISION
LINEAGE
    Constituted 18 July 1917 in the National Guard as Headquarters, 26th Division. Organized 22 August 1917 at Boston, Massachusetts with troops from Connecticut, Maine, Massachusetts, New Hampshire, Rhode Island, and Vermont. Demobilized 3 May 1919 at Camp Devens, Massachusetts.
CAMPAIGN PARTICIPATION
    World War I
        Champagne-Marne
        Aisne-Marne
        St. Mihiel
        Meuse-Argonne
        Ile-de-France 1918
        Lorraine 1918
Approved: 26 October 1918

    On 23 October 1918 Headquarters 26th Division by telegram to Adj't. General, General Headquarters, A.E.F. "Number four eight seven period Retel M-674 period distinctive cloth design adopted by twenty sixth division colon YD comma in monogram comma in blue cloth color of french uniform period sample follows by mail." On 26 October 1918 by telegram of G.H.Q., A.E.F. to Commanding General, 26th Division "Number M-738. Reference your telegram Number Four eight seven comma design adopted as insignia for 26th Division is approved." On 2 November 1918 by ORDERS No. 213 Headquarters 26th Division wrote: "I. In accordance with orders from General Headquarters, Am. E. F., all officers and enlisted men of this division will wear the following distinguishing insignia on their left shoulder: A diamond on khaki cloth, 4 inches long and 3 ½ inches wide, with the initials YD in dark blue superimposed. The upper point of the insignia will be attached to the shoulder seam." A sketch of the insignia was depicted on the order.

Symbolism: The "Y D" alludes to the division's nickname, "Yankee Division."

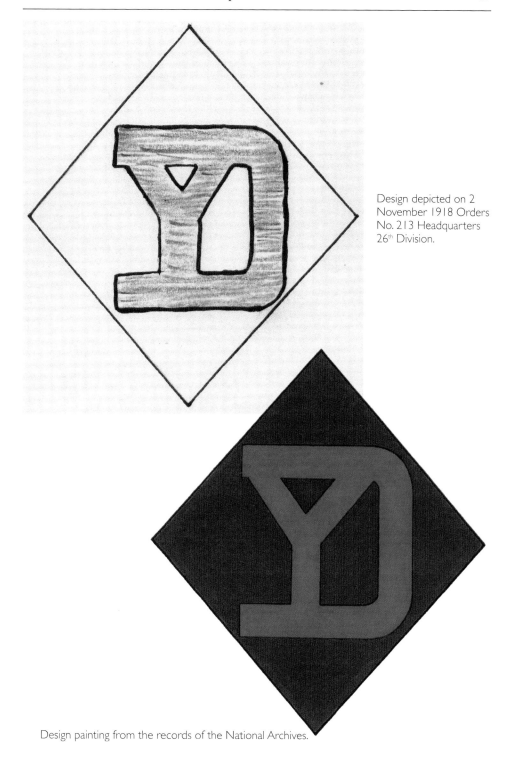

Design depicted on 2 November 1918 Orders No. 213 Headquarters 26th Division.

Design painting from the records of the National Archives.

TWENTY-SEVENTH DIVISION
LINEAGE

Constituted 9 February 1898 in the New York National Guard as Headquarters, New York Division and organized at Albany, New York. Disbanded 4 April 1898 and reconstituted 23 June 1908. Redesignated 28 June 1916 as Headquarters, 6th Division and mustered into federal service at New York and mustered out 23 December 1916 at New York. Mustered into federal service 16 July 1917 at Camp Whitman, New York; drafted into federal service 5 August 1917. Redesignated 1 October 1917 as Headquarters, 27th Division. Demobilized 1 April 1919 at Camp Upton, New York.

CAMPAIGN PARTICIPATION

World War I:
    Ypres-Lys
    Somme Offensive
Approved: 29 October 1918

On 19 October 1918 Commanding General, 27th Division wrote Adjutant General, American E.F. "1. In compliance with telegram No. M674 and in continuation of our telegram No. G-1/675, inclosed find design of 27th Division insignia for approval." By telegram of G.H.Q., A.E.F. 29 October 1918 to Commanding General, 27th Division advised "Number M-761. Reference your letter of October nineteenth comma design adopted as insignia for 27th Division is approved."

On 26 May 1922, a memorandum from War Department General Staff to the Adjutant General of the Army stated "The Secretary of War directs that the drawing herewith be sent to the Quartermaster General, together with a communication in substance as follows: "The shoulder sleeve insignia of the 27th Division is described as follows: On a black disc 2 1/2" in diameter the monogram "N.Y." with all members 1/8" wide and the constellation of Orion of seven stars all in red within a red circle 2 1/4" in diameter and 1/8" in width."

Symbolism: The letters "NY" in the form of a monogram represent the state of New York. The seven stars suggest the constellation of Orion, which alludes to the name of the division's WWI commanding general, Major General John F. O'Ryan.

Drawing believed to be that inclosed with 19 October communication of Commanding General, 27th Division to Adjutant General, G.H.Q., American E.F.

TWENTY-EIGHTH DIVISION
LINEAGE
   Organized 12-20 March 1879 at Philadelphia as Headquarters, Division of the Pennsylvania National Guard. Mustered into federal service 29 June 1916 as Headquarters, 7th Division; mustered out 23 February 1917 at Philadelphia. Drafted into federal service 5 August 1917 and redesignated 1 September 1917 as Headquarters, 28th Division. Demobilized 17 May 1919 at Camp Dix, New Jersey.
CAMPAIGN PARTICIPATION CREDIT
   World War I
         Champagne-Marne
         Aisne-Marne
         Oise-Aisne
         Meuse-Argonne
         Champagne 1918
         Lorraine 1918.
Approved: 19 October 1918

   On 19 October 1918 by telegram of 28th Division to G.H.Q., A.E.F. the 28th Division requested approval of a red keystone as the distinctive insignia of the division. On the same date G.H.Q., A.E.F. replied by telegram to Commanding General, 28th Division "M-682 Reference you telegram October 19th adoption of red keystone as insignia your division approved." On 22 October 1918 Headquarters 28th Division wrote to C. G., Hq., American E. F. a memorandum "Reference to your No. 280, the insignia as authorized for this Division is a cloth Keystone in solid red, dimensions and design as per sample attached." The sketch of the sample of the attached insignia was 2 1/4" in height, the top 1 11/16" wide, the widest section 2 1/8", the base 15/16" wide. On 24 October 1918 the memorandum from General Headquarters American Expeditionary Forces setting forth "...the Divisions which have submitted descriptions of the distinctive insignia adopted, and which have been approved by this office,..." described the design as: "Red Keystone." On 27 October 1918, a memorandum of Headquarters 28th Division entitled "MEMORANDUM – RED KEYSTONE. A RED KEYSTONE has been designated as the distinctive insignia of this Division. Keystones are to be worn on all coats and overcoats, including the trench and short coats worn by officers, and the mackinaws issued to Engineers, motorcycle drivers, etc., but not on the slicker. A standard size of Keystone of selected color and quality of cloth has been adopted and contracted for by the Quartermaster's Department. These will be issued at the rate of two per man and no others will be worn. They are to be sewed on the left sleeve with red thread, the top to be on the line of the seam. The proportions of a keystone are shown below:" (See design below.)
   By an undated communication (a script date of 6/21/22 appears in lower right of the memo, and also noted is 1 incl. (drawing)) from the Adjutant General by order of the Secretary of War to the Quartermaster General the following was written: "1. The shoulder sleeve insignia of the 28th Division was approved by telegram October 19, 1918, from the Adjutant General, A.E. F., to Commanding General, 28th Division, It is described as follows: A red keystone approximately 2 – 1/4" in height and 2" in width."

Symbolism: The keystone, symbol of the state of Pennsylvania, alludes to the
nickname of the division, "Keystone Division."

Design drawing inclosed with 22 October 1918
communication of Headquarters Twenty-Eighth
Division to C.G., Hq., American E.F.

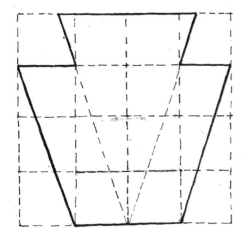

Design depicted on 27 October 1918
MEMORANDUM – RED KEYSTONE of
Headquarters 28th Division showing the
proportions of the Keystone.

Design painting from the records of the
National Archives.

TWENTY-NINTH DIVISION
LINEAGE
Constituted 18 July 1917 in the National Guard as Headquarters, 29th Division. Organized 25 August 1917 at Camp McClellan, Alabama with troops from Delaware, Maryland, New Jersey, Virginia and the District of Columbia. Demobilized 30 May 1919 at Camp Dix, New Jersey.
CAMPAIGN PARTICIPATION
World War I
Meuse-Argonne
Alsace 1918
Approved: 21 October 1918

On 20 October 1918 Headquarters 29th Division replied by telegram to Adjutant General, HAEF advising " RETEL OCTOBER NINETEENTH NUMBER M SIX SEVEN FOUR RELATIVE TO DISTINCTIVE CLOTH DESIGN TO BE WORN BY OFFICERS AND MEN OF THE DIVISION PERIOD KOREAN LUCKY SYMBOL WHICH IS THE SAME TRADE MARK USED BY THE NORTHERN PACIFIC RAILWAY COMMA COLORS BLUE AND GRAY WAS ADOPTED BY THIS DIVISION ONE YEAR AGO IN UNITED STATES PERIOD REQUEST APPROVAL OF THIS DESIGN." By telegram from G.H.Q., A.E.F. to Commanding General 29th Division of 21 October 1918 wrote "NUMBER M-695 REFERENCE YOUR TELEGRAM OF OCTOBER TWENTIETH DESIGN ADOPTED BY 29TH DIVN IS APPROVED PERIOD SUBMIT BY MAIL SAMPLE DESIGN OR DRAWING AND COMPLETE DESCRIPTION THEREOF FOR RECORD OF THESE HEADQUARTERS." On 23 October Hq. 29th Division by a 1st Ind. wrote to The adjutant General, G.H.Q., A.E.F. "1. Sample design is submitted herewith. 2. The design for this division is the Korean lucky symbol, which is also the symbol used by the Northern Pacific Railway in the United States. The left half of the symbol is blue, and the right half is gray." By letter of 5 November 1918 Commanding General, First Army advised Commanding General, 29th Division "1. The C. in C. has approved the following shoulder insignia for your division: Korean lucky symbol, same as trademark used by Northern Pacific Railway."

By Bulletin No. 126. of HEADQUARTERS 29TH DIVISION of 15 Nov. 1918 advised "I. 1. The following design of shoulder insignia for this division has been approved: Korean lucky symbol, now in use as insignia of this division. 2. The insignia will be two inches in diameter and will be worn on the left shoulder with top of the insignia at the shoulder seam of sleeve of coat with the blue sector to the front. …"

A memorandum dated 16 June 1922 from War Department General Staff to the Adjutant General of the Army stated "The Secretary of War directs that the drawing herewith be sent to the Quartermaster General, together with a communication in substance as follows: The shoulder sleeve insignia of the 29th Division was approved by telegram dated October 21, 1918 from the Adjutant General, American Expeditionary Forces, to Commanding General, 29th Division. It is described as follows: Upon a disc 2 – 1/4" in diameter a tah gook the curves being circles of half the radius of the disc. The heraldic dexter half being gray and the sinister half blue."

Symbolism: In 1918, the division was formed with two National Guard units from the North and from the South. Therefore, the North is represented by the blue and the South by gray.

Design painting from the records
of the National Archives.

THIRTIETH DIVISION
LINEAGE
Constituted 18 July 1917 in the National Guard as Headquarters, 30th Division. Organized 28 August – 12 September 1917 at Camp Sevier, South Carolina with troops from North Carolina, South Carolina and Tennessee. Demobilized 7 May 1919 at Camp Jackson, South Carolina.
CAMPAIGN PARTICIPATION
World War I:
Somme Offensive
Ypres-Lys
Flanders 1918
Approved: 23 October 1918

On 19 October 1918 30th Division by telegram to G HQ AM E F Haef wrote "Cs 56 19 AAA division distinctive cloth design to be elliptical maroon cloth two and three fourths inches by one and three fourths inches AAA Further design in blue to be superimposed later AAA This additional design too complicated to describe by telegram but is being forwarded by letter and will be added later if approved AAA The entire design is the divisional insignia adopted several months ago AAA Will the cloth design be furnished this division by British or American supply depot question". On 20 October 1918 Commanding General 30th Division wrote to Commander–in-Chief, American Expeditionary Forces "1. Complete distinctive cloth design to be worn by the officers and men of this division is forwarded herewith for approval. The blue design is to be superimposed upon the maroon design referred to telegram C.S. – 56, these Headquarters, dated October 19th. The practicability of this design depends upon the ability of the supply department to furnish the superimposed blue cloth design. It is desired to retain it if possible, as it has been in use on all Division Transport, etc. for several months. The O.H. stands for "Old Hickory" and the XXX for 30th Division." On 23 October 1918 the Adjutant General, American Expeditionary Forces wrote Commanding General, 30th Division "1. Reference your letter of October 20, 1918, the design inclosed therein has been approved by the Commander-in-Chief as the insignia for 30th Division. 2. The question as to the ability of the supply department to furnish this design is a matter which should be taken up with the Chief Quartermaster." On 24 October 1918 the memorandum from General Headquarters, American Expeditionary Forces setting forth "…the Divisions which have submitted descriptions of the distinctive insignia adopted, and which have been approved by this office,…" described the design as: "Monogram, letter "O" surrounding letter "H", with three "X"s inside the cross-bar of the "H"; on maroon cloth. OH stands for Old Hickory, and the three Xs for 30th."

By a 1st Ind. of 22 February 1919 Commanding General, 30th Division to Commanding General, S.O.S. American E.F. wrote in part "1. The divisional insignia of the 30th Division was adopted and used on the divisional transport as early as June 1918. Therefore, when G.H.Q. directed, in October, that a distinctive divisional insignia be adopted and worn by all officers and men of the division, this design was submitted to G.H.Q. and approved by the Commander-in-Chief. 2. The design is a monogram in blue, the letter "O" surrounding the letter "H", with three X's inside the cross-bar of the letter "H", all of which is superimposed upon a maroon cloth, thus:" (Design is depicted in color on the 1st Ind.)

On 16 June 1922, a memorandum from War Department General Staff to the Adjutant General of the Army stated "The Secretary of War directs that the drawing herewith be sent to the Quartermaster General, together with a communication in substance as follows: "The shoulder sleeve insignia of the 30th Division was approved by letter dated October 23, 1918 from the Adjutant General, American Expeditionary Forces, to Commanding General, 30th Division. It is described as follows: The letters "O H" blue upon a red background, the "O" forming the elliptical outline of the device long axis to be 2 – 1/2" and short axis 1 – 5/8". The letter "H" within the "O". The letters "XXX" on the bar of the "H". The letters "O H" are the initials of "Old Hickory" and the "XXX" is the Roman notation for the number of the Division. When this patch was first issued in France it was inadvertently worn with the long axis horizontally, and the custom of so wearing has continued." On 25 March 1922 Colonel Oliver L. Spalding (formerly Brigadier General, Commanding 55th F. A. Brigade) reported that "It has been the custom in the division for the artillery to wear the shoulder mark vertically instead of horizontally, as the rest of the division does." "When the mark was adopted, the artillery brigade was serving detached from the division…" and "I directed that it be worn vertically, this seeming the natural way." On sheet 5-2-7 of the Office Quartermaster General dated 20 January 1923 the design is shown horizontally. It is reported it was worn both ways until 1941.

Symbolism: The letters "O" and "H" are the initials of the division nickname "Old Hickory," and the "XXX" is the Roman numeral of the division's numerical designation

Sample in approval records of the National Archives.

Drawing depicted on 22 February 1919 1st Indorsement of Headquarters 30th Division to Commanding General, S.O.S., American E.F.

THIRTY-FIRST DIVISION
LINEAGE
Constituted 18 July 1917 in the National Guard as Headquarters, 31st Division. Organized 25 August 1917 at Camp Wheeler, Georgia with troops from Alabama, Florida and Georgia. Demobilized 14 January 1919 at Camp Gordon, Georgia..
CAMPAIGN PARTICIPATION
World War I
Streamer without inscription
Approved: 7 March 1919

On 25 October 1918 by telegram CHIEF OF STAFF 31st Division, to ADJT GENERAL A E F wrote "REFERENCE TELEGRAM NUMBER M SIX FIVE FOUR DESIGN FOR THIRTY FIRST DIVISION CONSISTS OF TWO LETTERS D COMMA THE FIRST D INVERTED LATERALLY COMMA SURROUNDED BY A CIRCLE COMMA INDICATION THE DIXIE DIVISION PERIOD THIS NAME AND EMBLEM WERE OFFICIALLY ADOPTED IN NINETEEN SEVENTEEN PERIOD DESIGN FOLLOWS BY MAIL." In follow up on same date Commanding General, 31st Division to Adjutant General, A.E.F. wrote "Reference your telegram dated 22 October, No. M-654, there is attached copy of telegram dated 25 October, 1918, giving information as to the distinctive design for the 31st Division. There is attached copy of the design, and approval is requested." A copy of Memorandum No. 129 of Headquarters 31st division of 27 March 1918 depicting the design was attached.

On 7 March 1919 a letter from Adjutant General, General Headquarters, American Expeditionary Forces, to Col. C. B. Hodges, Inf. (Formerly Act. Chief of Staff, 31st Div.) wrote "The divisional symbol adopted for the 31st Division by Memorandum 129, Headquarters 31st Division, Camp Wheeler, March 27, 1918 has been made of record in the A. E. F. as the distinctive insignia for the 31st Division. The memorandum above noted has been retained at these Headquarters for the purpose of record."

On 7 July 1922, a memorandum from War Department General Staff for the Adjutant General of the Army stated "The Secretary of War directs that the drawing herewith be sent to the Quartermaster General, together with a communication in substance as follows: The shoulder sleeve insignia of the 31st Division was approved by letter March 7, 1919 from the Adjutant General, A. E. F., to Commanding General 31st Division. It is described as follows: Within a red circle 2 – 1/2 inches in diameter and 3/16 of an inch in width on a white disc the red letters DD back to back in the form of an octagon, elements if the letters 1/8 inch in width."

Symbolism: The two "D"s allude to the division's nickname, "Dixie Division."

Drawing inclosed with 25 October 1918 communication of Commanding General, 31ˢᵗ Division to the Adjutant General, A.E.F. Design conforms to that depicted in Division Memorandum No.129 of 27 March 1918. (Note: drawing is 2 ½ inches in diameter per descriptions, although original inclosure of 25 October 1918 was 4 15/16 inches.)

Design painting from the records of the National Archives.

THIRTY-SECOND DIVISION
LINEAGE
    Constituted 18 July 1917 in the National Guard as Headquarters, 32nd Division. Organized 4 August 1917 at Camp MacArthur, Texas with troops from Michigan and Wisconsin. Demobilized 23 May 1919 at Camp Custer, Michigan
CAMPAIGN PARTICIPATION
    World War I
        Aisne-Marne
        Oise-Aisne
        Meuse-Argonn
        Alsace
        Champagne
Approved: 11 November 1918

    On 20 October 1918 Commanding General, 32nd Division submitted to Adjutant General, 1st Army, American Expeditionary Forces a letter "In compliance with telegram from Headquarters First Army, A. E. F., dated 18 October 1918, reference insignia for divisions, there is submitted herewith design for the distinguishing insignia this Division." By 1st Ind. of 28 October 1918 Headquarters First Army forwarded the letter to Commander-in-Chief, G.H.Q.A.E.F. recommending approval. By 2nd Ind. of 2 November from G.H.Q., American E.F. to Commanding General, 32nd Division (Through C.G., 1st Army) replied "1. Returned. The insignia submitted can not be approved on account of its similarity to the insignia previously approved for the 35th Division. 2. It is desired that another design be selected by your division and submitted to this office for consideration." By 4th Ind. of 6 November 1918 HQ. 32nd Division to Commanding General, First Army wrote "1. The 2nd Ind. has been noted and, in conformity thereto, the attached design for shoulder distinguishing insignia is submitted for that previously forwarded and is submitted for approval. 2. It is requested that these Headquarters be notified by wire if this symbol is approved." By telegram of 11 November 1918 G.H.Q., A.E.F. advised Commanding General, 32d Division "Number M-842. Reference your fourth indorsement of November sixth comma design submitted as insignia for thirty-second Division is approved." On 22 November 1918 Commanding General, 32nd Division advised "The accompanying sketch illustrates the manner in which the new Divisional insignia is to be worn. To be sewn on the left shoulder with the top of arrow 1/4 inch from the shoulder seam of coat sleeve." The design was "A red arrow 3 1/4" in length "having shot through a line"." G.H.Q., A.E.F. approved the insignia 11 November 1918. Reportedly the Commanding General, 32nd Division, Major General Wm. Haan, stated "I chose the Barred-Arrow as the Division symbol because we pierced every line the Boche put before us."." On the "LIST OF DIVISIONAL INSIGNIAS APPROVED BY GHQ TO DATE" by Office Chief Q.M. AEF of Jan. 1, 1919 the description is "Red arrow with cross bar in center."
    On 26 May 1922, a memorandum from War Department General Staff for the Adjutant General of the Army stated "The Secretary of War directs that the drawing herewith be sent to the Quartermaster General, together with a communication in substance as follows: The shoulder sleeve insignia of the 32nd Division is described as follows: A red arrow 3 1/4" in length "having shot through a line." "

Symbolism: The red arrow piercing a line was selected because they "shot thru
           every line the Boche put up."

Sample in approval records of the
National Archives believed to be
that forwarded with 6 November
1918 4th Ind.

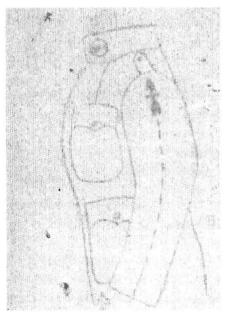

Drawing in 22 November 1918 communication
of Commanding General, 32nd Division
illustrating how the Divisional insignia is to be
worn.

Design painting from the records of the
National Archives.

THIRTY-THIRD DIVISION
LINEAGE

Constituted from 12th National Guard Division of the Illinois National Guard and renumbered as 33rd Division. Activated 17 July 1917 at Camp Logan, Texas and organized 27 August 1917. Demobilized May 1919

CAMPAIGN PARTICIPATION

World War I

Meuse-Argonne

Somme

St. Mihiel

Approved: 21 October 1918

On 19 October 1918 Commanding General, 33rd Division wrote Chief of Staff, First Army "1. In compliance with the attached telegram, enclosed herewith is suggested design for distinguishing insignia for the 33rd Division. 2. This design has been used on the transportation, boxes and other marks of this Division for the last year. If it is considered that the two pieces of cloth would be too complex to manufacture, then the yellow cross is recommended." On 20 October Commanding General, 33rd Division by telegram to ADJUTANT GENERAL GHQAEF wrote "G-1-409 PERIOD RETEL NUMBER M 474 THIS DIVISION HAS ADOPTED A DESIGN OF A YELLOW CROSS ON A BLACK CIRCULAR BACKGROUND TWO INCHES IN DIAMETER PERIOD DRAWINGS HAVE BEEN MADE AND FORWARDED TO THE FIRST ARMY IN ACCORDANCE WITH THEIR DIRECTIONS PERIOD THIS DESIGN HAS BEEN THE INSIGNIA OF THIS DIVISION SINCE ITS ORIGINATION IN MARKING ITS BOXES AND WAGONS PERIOD". On 21 October 1918 G.H.Q., A.E.F. to Commanding General, 33rd Division by telegram advised "Number M-697. Reference your telegram G-1-409 comma design adopted by 33rd Division is approved period Submit by mail sample of design or drawing and complete description thereof for records of these Headquarters." In General Orders No. 143 of Headquarters 33rd Division, paragraph "III. DIVISIONAL INSIGNIA 1. In compliance with telegraphic instructions, H.A.E.F., wire number M-674 and under authority of wire Number M-697, H.A.E.F., all officers and men of this Division will wear the <u>distinguishing insignia</u> of this Division in cloth on the left arm, the upper part thereof to be attached to the shoulder seam, 2. The insignia of the Division is a yellow cross on a black circular background two inches in diameter, the official design of which is on file in the office of the Division Adjutant. 3. The Division Quartermaster will procure a supply of the insignia."

In a MEMORANDUM FOR THE ADJUTANT GENERAL OF THE ARMY from the War Department General Staff dated June 21, 1922 the insignia was described as follows: "On a black disc 2 – 1/4" in diameter a yellow greek cross 1 – 3/4" in height and breadth with arms 1/2" in width."

Symbolism: Yellow cross adopted from equipment marking used in the Philippines during the Spanish-American War to avoid theft by tribesman who were superstitious of yellow crosses (*see opposite page*).

THIRTY-FOURTH DIVISION
LINEAGE
Constituted 18 July 1917 in the National Guard as Headquarters, 34th Division. Organized 25 August 1917 at Camp Cody, New Mexico with troops from Iowa, Minnesota, Nebraska, North Dakota, and South Dakota. Demobilized 18 February 1919 at Camp Grant, Illinois.
CAMPAIGN PARTICIPATION
World War I
Streamer without inscription
Approved: 29 October 1918

On 23 October 1918 Commanding General, 34th Division by telegram wrote Adjutant General, HAEF "NUMBER 47 REFERENCE YOUR TELEGRAM OCTOBER FIFTEENTH RECOMMEND DEVICE FOR THIS DIVISION ALREADY ADOPTED BE APPROVED AS DISTINCTIVE CLOTH DESIGN TO BE WORN ON LEFT SHOULDER PERIOD DESCRIPTION COMMA SKULL OF STEER WITH HORNS FRONT VIEW MADE OF RED CLOTH SEWED ON OVAL PATCH OF BLACK CLOTH PERIOD DEVICE IS SYMBOLIC OF DESERT COUNTRY FROM WHICH THIS DIVISION CAME PERIOD SKETCH MAILED YOU TODAY". On same date Commanding General, 34th Division wrote Commanding General, General Headquarters, A.E.F. "1. In compliance with your telegram of 15 October, 1918, a telegraphic report of the design recommended for adoption as a distinctive shoulder mark of this Division was made this date. 2. The enclosed sketch of the design is forwarded for your information." On 29 October 1918 G.H.Q., A.E.F. by telegram to Commanding General 34th Division advised "Number M-758. Reference your letter of October twenty-third comma design adopted as insignia for 34th Division is approved." (The sketch enclosed with the 23 October 1918 communication was not found in the records of the National Archives or The Institute of Heraldry.)

On 27 June 1922, a memorandum from War Department General Staff to the Adjutant General of the Army stated "The Secretary of War directs that the drawing herewith be sent to the Quartermaster General, together with a communication in substance as follows: The shoulder sleeve insignia of the 34th Division was approved by telegram October 29th, 1918 from the Adjutant General, A. E. F. to the Commanding General, 34th Division. It is described as follows: On a black olla approximately 2 inches in width and 2 ¼ inches in height a red bull skull."

Symbolism: The patch shape simulates an olla (Mexican water flask), symbolizing the 34th Division's origin, formation, and intensive training site at Camp Cody, New Mexico, in October 1917. The bull skull also symbolizes the surrounding dry, desert-like area. Black denotes durability, firmness, and stability, and red is for courage and action.

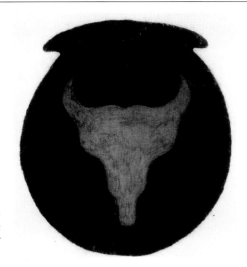

Design painting from the records of the National Archives. for the 34th Division.

THIRTY-FIFTH DIVISION
LINEAGE
Constituted 18 July 1917 in the National Guard as Headquarters, 35th Division. Organized 25 August 1917 at Camp Doniphan, Oklahoma with troops from Kansas and Missouri. Demobilized 26 May 1919 at Camp Funston, Kansas.
CAMPAIGN PARTICIPATION
World War I
        Meuse-Argonne
        Alsace 1918
        Lorraine 1918
Approved: 29 October 1918

On 21 October 1918 Commanding General, 35th Division, telegrammed ADJ GEN HAEF: "IN RE YOUR TELEGRAM M- -674 THE DESIGN 35TH DIVN IS THE SANTAFE CROSS NOW MARKED ON TRANSPORTATION IN DIFFERENT COLORS FOR DIFFERENT UNITS PERIOD THIS WILL BE ISSUED IN DIFFERENT COLORS FOR DIFFERENT UNITS IF APPROVED AT YOUR HEADQUARTERS PERIOD A CHART SHOWING SAME WILL BE FOWARDED BY MAIL IF DESIRED". On 22 October G.H.Q., A.E.F. responded by telegram to "Commanding General, 35th Division Number M-705 Reference your telegram of October twenty-first comma submit sample or drawing of design with complete description period Upon receipt of this comma decision as to approval will be made." By letter on 23 October 1918 from Commanding General, 35th Division to The Adjutant General, G.H.Q., A.E.F. wrote:
        Subject: Designs for Division symbol to be worn on left shoulder.
                1. Enclosed herewith is a drawing illustrating the design which it is desired to use for the symbols to be worn on the left arm just below the shoulder seam. The variations in color are according to a definite plan"
                2 incl.

SYMBOLS FOR ALL ORGANIZATIONS OF THE 35TH DIVISION

Division Headquarters	4/4 blue	Circle	blue
Headquarters Troop	3/4 blue, 1/4 yellow	Circle	blue
69 th Inf. Brig.Hq.	4/4 yellow	Circle	yellow
137 th Reg. Infantry	3/4 yellow, 1/4 blue	Circle	yellow
138 th Reg. Infantry	2/4 yellow, 2/4 blue	Circle	yellow
70 th Inf. Brig. Hq.	4/4 black	Circle	black
139 th Reg. Infantry	3/4 black, 1/4 yellow	Circle	black
140 th Reg. Infantry	2/4 black, 2/4 yellow	Circle	black
110 th Reg. Engrs.	4/4 white	Circle	white
110 th Engr. Tn.	3/4 white, 1/4 red	Circle	white
110 th Fd. Sig. Bn.	4/4 green	Circle	green
60 th Fd. Arty. Brig. Hq.	4/4 red	Circle	red
128 th Reg. Fd. Arty.	3/4 red, 1/4 blue	Circle	red
129 th Reg. Fd. Arty.	3/4 red, 1/4 yellow	Circle	red
130 th Reg. Fd. Arty.	3/4 red, 1/4 white	Circle	red
Train Hq. & M.P.	4/4 maroon	Circle	green
110 th Sanitary Train	3/4 maroon, 1/4 green	Circle	green
110 th Supply Train	3/4 maroon, 1/4 yellow	Circle	green
110 th Ammunition Train	3/4 maroon, 1/4 white	Circle	green
128 th M.G.Bn.	3/4 blue, 1/4 green	Circle	blue
129 th M.G.Bn.	2/4 red, 2/4 yellow, alternate	Circle	yellow
130th M.G.Bn.	2/4 black, 2/4 yellow, alternate	Circle	black
110 th Trench Mor.Btry.	3/4 red, 1/4 green	Circle	red

Design drawings accompanying 23 October 1918 communication of Commanding General, 35th Division to The Adjutant General, G.H.Q., A.E.F. depicting designs for the Division HQ., 128th REG. F.A., and 140th REG. INF.

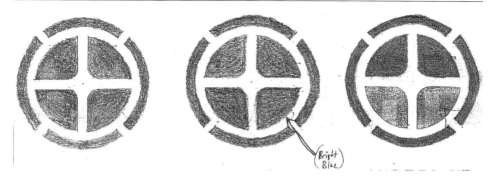

Copy of design drawings accompanying 23 October 1918 communication of Commanding General, 35ᵗʰ Division to The Adjutant General, G.H.Q., A.E.F. depicting designs for the Division HQ., 128ᵗʰ REG. F.A., and 140ᵗʰ REG. INF. With the notations Division HQ "drawn in bright blue pencil"; 128ᵗʰ REG.F.A. "drawn in bright red pencil, except for lower right quadrant in bright blue pencil"; and 140ᵗʰ REG. INF. "drawn in black pencil, except lower quadrants, which are pieces of buff-colored paper glued to the page."

On 29 October 1918 G.H.Q., A.E.F. to Commanding General, 35ᵗʰ Division telegrammed "Number M-760. Reference your letter of October 23rd comma design adopted as insignia for 35ᵗʰ Division is approved." On 14 November, in General Orders No. 34 of Headquarters First Army the insignia was described as "Santa Fe cross (different colors for the several organizations."

On 7 June 1922, a memorandum for the Adjutant General from the War Department General Staff wrote "The secretary of War directs that the drawing herewith be sent to the Quartermaster General, together with a communication in substance as follows: The shoulder sleeve insignia of the 35ᵗʰ Division was approved by telegram October 29, 1918, from the Adjutant General, A.E.F., to Commanding General, 35ᵗʰ Division. It is described as follows: Within a blue circle 2" in diameter, 1/8" in width quadrated at 45 degrees to the lines of disc, a blue quadrated disc 1 1/2" in diameter, the inner ends of the quadrants rounded by arcs of 1/8" radius, all white lines 1/8" in width."

Symbolism: The Santa Fe cross was a symbol used to mark the old Santa Fe trail, an area where the unit trained, and was officially designated as an identifying device for the unit. The organization is referred to as the Santa Fe Division.

Design painting from the records of the National Archives.

The following 23 sketch drawings are representative of the "SYMBOLS FOR ALL ORGANIZATIONS OF THE 35TH DIVISION" as listed in the inclosure to the communication of 23 October 1918 of Commanding General, 35th Division to The Adjutant General, G.H.Q., A.E.F. Note that the color pattern is based on the design drawings described above. It is recognized that these patterns do not correspond with other printed depictions of these insignia, nor as they were worn by all troops; however, research indicates they are consistent with the intent of the approval records.

Division Headquarters.

Headquarters Troop.

69th Infantry Brigade Headquarters.

137th Infantry Regiment.

138th Infantry Regiment.

70th Infantry Brigade. Headquarters.

139th Infantry Regiment.

140th Infantry Regiment.

110th Engineer Regiment.

110th Engineer.Train.

110th Field Signal Battalion.

60th Field Artillery Brigade Headquarters.

128th Field Artillery Regiment.

129th Field Artillery Regiment.

130th Field Artillery Regiment.

110th Train Headquarters & Military Police.

110th Sanitary Train.

110th Supply Train.

110th Ammunition Train.

128th Machine Gun Battalion.

129th Machine Gun Battalion.

130th Machine Gun Battalion.

110th Trench Mortar Battery.

THIRTY-SIXTH DIVISION

LINEAGE

Constituted 18 July 1917 in the National Guard as Headquarters, 36th Division. Organized 23 August 1917 at Camp Bowie, Texas with troops from Oklahoma and Texas. Demobilized 18 June 1919 at Camp Bowie, Texas.

CAMPAIGN PARTICIPATION

World War I

Meuse-Argonne

Approved: 12 November 1918

On 21 October 1918 Commanding General, 36th Division by telegram to C. IN C. GHQ HAEF wrote "REFERENCE YOUR TELEGRAM DIRECTING DIVISIONS ADOPT DISTINCTIVE CLOTH DESIGN TO BE WORN ON LEFT UPPER ARM COMMA THE THIRTY SIXTH DIVISION HAS ADOPTED A FIVE POINTED STAR DISTINCTIVE OF THE LONE STAR STATE AND ALSO THE FLAG OF OKLAHOMA". On the same date G.H.Q., A.E.F. replied to Commanding General, 36th Division by telegram "M-704. Reference your telegram October twenty-first comma submit sample or drawing of design selected with complete description as to color and size period Upon receipt of this comma decision as to approval will be made period". On 23 October The Commanding General, 36th Division wrote The Commander in Chief, G.H.Q., A.E.F. "1. In compliance with your telegram No. M704, dated October 21st, I am submitting herewith drawing of the distinctive badge which is desired shall be adopted to be worn on the upper left arm of members of the 36th Division. The circular piece of cloth is to be of the regular Olive Drab material, three and one-quarter inches in diameter, with a blue, five pointed star in the center, distance from opposite points of the star to be two and one-half inches. 2. This division was formed of National Guard Troops from the States of Texas and Oklahoma. Texas has long been known as The Lone star State, and the flag of Oklahoma contains a single large star. It is believed, therefore, that the adoption of the above described distinctive badge would be proper and fitting." On 6 November 1918 G.H.Q., A.E.F. by telegram to Commanding General, 36th Division advised "Number M-810. Reference your letter of October twenty-third comma design submitted as insignia for 36th Division cannot be approved on account of similarity to approved design of 2d Division period Another design will be selected and reported by wire to this office for consideration comma sample or drawing with complete description thereof to be sent by mail for records of these Headquarters."

On 9 November 1918 by telegram Commanding General, 36th Division to ADJ GEN, AEF wrote "RETEL YOUR NUMBER M EIGHT ONE NAUGHT PERIOD FOLLOWING IS SUBMITTED AS NOW DISTINCTIVE INSIGNIA FOR THIS DIVISION COLON KHAKI DISK THREE AND FIVE EIGHTS INCHES IN DIAMETER IN WHICH IS AN IRREGULAR EDGED BLUE ARROW HEAD PERIOD WITHIN THE ARROW HEAD IS A KHAKI BLOCKED LETTER T PERIOD DRAWING AND COMPLETE DIMENSION FORWARDED PERIOD". By letter of the same date Commanding General, 36th Division wrote to The Adjutant General, American E F "1. Attached hereto is sample and complete description of the new design submitted as a distinctive insignia emblem for the 36th Division. The arrow head is representative of the State of Oklahoma and the blocked letter "T" the State of Texas, from which states the men of this command come. Particular attention is invited to the irregular edge of the arrow head, which should be preserved." By telegram of 12 November 1918 GHQ, AEF replied to Commanding General, 36th Division "M-848 Reference letter November ninth comma design for insignia your division as submitted approved."

In an extract of Memorandum No. 24 of Headquarters, 36th Division on 16 January 1919 the division insignia was described as "The distinctive Division Insignia for the 36th Division is a circular disk, olive drab cloth, 85/10 cm. in diameter upon which is superimposed an arrowhead of cobalt blue, length of arrow head is 7 5/10cm width of arrow head 4 2/10cm. arrowhead pointing down. Within the arrowhead is a block letter "T" of olive drab cloth, 3 3/10 cm., in length; 2 2/4 cm., in width; width of stem is 0.6 cm. This insignia is worn on the sleeve of the left arm, dropped one inch from the top of the Arm seam with the coat; the insignia being sewed on the sleeve in such position that the arrowhead, pointing downward, will be in prolongation of the shoulder strap of the coat. No members of this command will be allowed to wear the Division Insignia of colors other than herein described, namely the regulation olive drab cloth for the circular disk and "T" and cobalt blue for the arrow head. The attempt to designate different arms of service by different colors in the Division Insignia is not in accordance with regulations and will not be worn."

Symbolism: The arrowhead alludes to the Indian territory of Oklahoma and the
              letter "T" to Texas.

Drawing inclosed with 22 February 1919 communication of A. C. of S., G-2, 36th Division to The Commanding General, S.O.S.

Design painting from the records of the National Archives. With notation "Arrow head should be irregular. No official design submitted."

THIRTY-SEVENTH DIVISION
LINEAGE
Constituted 18 July 1917 in the National Guard as Headquarters, 37th Division. Organized 26 August 1917 at Camp Sheridan, Alabama with troops from Ohio. Demobilized 23 June 1919 at Camp Sherman, Ohio.
CAMPAIGN PARTICIPATION
World War I
Ypres-Lys
Meuse-Argonne
Lorraine 1918
Approved: 5 November 1918

On 27 October 1918 G.H.Q., A.E.F. by telegram replied to a telegram from Commanding General, 37th Division "M-742. Reference your telegram October twenty-sixth comma send by mail sample or drawing of design period Upon receipt decision as to approval will be made period". On 29 October 1918 Commanding General, 37th Division wrote Adjutant General, American E. F. "1. In compliance with instructions contained in your telegram No. M 142, there is inclosed a sample drawing of the cloth design to be worn by each officer and man of the Division. This is the distinctive design adopted for this Division while in the United States and is painted on all transportation. Approval thereof is requested." The description was "Red circle with white border. Design adopted from the State flag of Ohio. Division known as the "Buckeye Division." By telegram of 5 November 1918 G.H.Q., A.E.F. replied to Commanding General, 37th Division "Number M-806. Reference your letter of October twenty-ninth comma design adopted by 37th Division is approved."

On 7 November 1918 Headquarters 37th Division issued a Bulletin No. 106, an extract of which stated "3. In accordance with telegraphic instructions from General Headquarters, American E. F., each Division will adopt a distinctive cloth design which will be worn by every officer and enlisted man of the Division on the left arm, upper part to be attached to the shoulder seam. The design adopted for this Division is a red circle 1 ½ inches in diameter with a white border 3/8 of an inch wide. Steps have been taken to procure a supply of these designs, and they are to be worn on the blouse and all coats."

On 26 May 1922, a memorandum from War Department General Staff to the Adjutant General of the Army stated "The Secretary of War directs that the drawing herewith be sent to the Quartermaster General, together with a communication in substance as follows: The shoulder sleeve insignia of the 37th Division is described as follows: On a white disc 2 ¼" in diameter a red disc 1 ½" in diameter."

Symbolism: The white disc superimposed by a red disc alludes to the "O" of Ohio, from which the troops forming the division came.

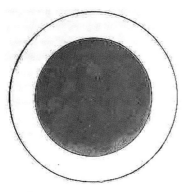

Drawing in approval records
of the National Archives.

Drawing in approval records illustrating how the Divisional insignia is to
be worn.

THIRTY-EIGHTH DIVISION
LINEAGE
Constituted 18 July 1917 in the National Guard as Headquarters, 38th Division. Organized 25 August 1917 at Camp Shelby, Mississippi with troops from Indiana, Kentucky, and West Virginia. Demobilized 8 March 1919 at Camp Zachary Taylor, Kentucky. (38th Division was formerly 17th Division.)
CAMPAIGN PARTICIPATION
World War I
Streamer without inscription
Approved: 30 October 1918

On 26 October 1918 Commanding General, 38th Division by telegram advised Headquarters A E F "RE TEL M 674 OCTOBER 20 TH COLON DESIGN ADOPTED FOR THIS DIVISION IS NAVY BLUE SHIELD 2 BY 2 INCHES WITH SUPERIMPOSED RED DIAMOND 1 1/4 IN VERTICLE BY 7/8 INCHES TRANSVERSE SECOND CHOICE SHIELD 2 BY 2 INCHES LEFT HALF NAVY BLUE RIGHT HALF RED SUPERIMPOSED INTERLACED LETTERS C Y IN WHITE EMBLEMATIC OF NAME CYCLONE DIVISION DRAWINGS BY MAIL". By letter of same date Commanding Officer, 149 Infantry, 38th Division wrote Commander in Chief, G.H.Q., A.E.F. "1. Pursuant to telegraphic instructions H.A.E.F., dated October 20, 1918, the following recommendations of designs for a distinctive cloth emblem to be worn on the left sleeve of each member of the Division are submitted. The first design described is the first choice of the Division; the second to be made use of in event the first cannot be approved on account of duplication: (a) Shield 2" wide x 2" long, navy blue; artillery red diamond 1 1/4" vertical x 7/8" transverse, superimposed in exact center of shield. Design to be worn with the straight side of shield attached to the shoulder seam. (b) Second choice: Shield 2" wide x 2" long, left half navy blue, right half artillery red. Superimposed in exact center of shield a white initial letter "C", 1" vertical x 1" transverse, with small letter vertical "y" interlaced with lower limb of initial C. Letters in white. The letters "Cy" emblematic of the name adopted for the Division, viz: "Cyclone". 2. Copies inclosed herewith. Telegraphic report of designs sent October 26, 1918." By telegram from G.H.Q., A.E.F. of 30 October 1918 to Commanding General, 38th Division advised "Number M-770. Reference your letter of October twenty-sixth comma red diamond design has already been approved as insignia for another Division period Your second choice of shield with letters CY superimposed is approved as insignia for Thirty-eighth Division."

On 16 June 1922, a memorandum from War Department General Staff to the Adjutant General of the Army stated "The Secretary of War directs that the drawing herewith be sent to the Quartermaster General, together with a communication in substance as follows: The shoulder sleeve insignia of the 38th Division was approved by telegram October 30th, 1918 from the Adjutant General, A. E. F. to the Commanding General, 38th Division. It is described as follows: On a spade shaped shield 2 1/4" in width and 2 – 1/2" in height, the heraldic dexter half blue, the sinister half red, a monogram of the letters "C" and "Y" in white, the elements of the letters 1/8" in width."

Symbolism: The monogram letters "C Y" alludes to the nickname of the division, "Cyclone Division."

Design drawing Second choice inclosed with 26 October 1918 communication of Commanding Officer, 149th Infantry, 38th Division to Commander-in-Chief, G.H.Q., A.E.F.

Design painting from the records of the National Archives.

Design painting from the records of the National Archives.

THIRTY-NINTH DIVISION
LINEAGE
    Constituted 18 July 1917 in the National Guard as Headquarters, 39th Division. Organized 25 August 1917 at Camp Beauregard, Louisiana with troops from Arkansas, Louisiana and Mississippi. Demobilized 23 January 1919 at Camp Beauregard, Louisiana.
CAMPAIGN PARTICIPATION
    World War I
        Streamer without inscription
No distinctive design approved by G.H.Q., A.E.F.

FORTIETH DIVISION
LINEAGE

Constituted 18 July 1917 in the National Guard as Headquarters, 40th Division. Organized 25 August 1917 at Camp Kearny, Nevada with troops from Arizona, California, Colorado, New Mexico, and Utah. Demobilized 20 April 1919 at Camp Kearny, California. (40th Division formerly 19th Division.)

CAMPAIGN PARTICIPATION

World War I

Streamer without inscription

Approved 23 November 1918

On 11 November 1918 C. G., 40th Division wrote C. G., 1st Army "1. The following distinctive design to be worn on coat sleeve of all officers and men of the 40th Division, is submitted for your approval: A sun – diameter 4 centimeters; distance from point to point of rays 6.2 centimeters, on a patch of navy blue cloth 7.6 by 7.6 centimeters." By 1st Ind. of 14 November Headquarters First Army to Commander-in-Chief, G.H.Q., American E.F. wrote "1. Forwarded, recommending approval. 2. It will be noted that this is a Replacement Division." On 16 November 1918 G.H.Q., A.E.F. advised Commanding General, 40th Division by telegram "Number M-864. Reference your letter of November eleventh to Commanding General First Army relative insignia for Fortieth Division comma submit by mail to this office sample or drawing with complete description of design adopted period Upon receipt of this comma decision as to approval will be telegraphed you." In reply by letter of 17 November C. G.., 40th Division wrote C in C, A.E.F. "1 As requested in telegram number M 864, Headquarters American Expeditionary Forces, November 16th 1918, there is enclosed herewith a drawing together with complete description of distinctive insignia which it is desired to adopt for the 40th (Sunshine) Division. 2. It is requested that action taken on this matter be telegraphed to these headquarters." On 19 November 1918 Headquarters First Army by telegram wrote TO COMMANDING GENERAL FORTIETH DIVISION "AG-1059 PERIOD DISTINCTIVE INSIGNIA FOR SUNSHINE DIVISION TENTATIVELY APPROVED PERIOD". On 19 November Commanding General, Fortieth Division by telegram to Adjutant General, G.H.Q., A.E.F. advised "Telegram 317 reference design for distinctive insignia fortieth division unable obtain sky blue cloth period. Have substituted King's blue cloth. No change in design request confirmation and authority." In reply by telegram of 20 November G.H.Q, A.E.F. to Commanding General, 40th Division wrote "Number M-895. Reference your telegram 317 comma change of color of distinctive design approved." Subsequently, on 23 November by telegram G.H.Q., A.E.F. advised Commanding General 40th Division "M-915 Reference your letter of November seventeenth comma distinctive design of sun submitted as insignia for fortieth Division is approved period". On 19 February 1919 Adjutant General, G.H.Q., A.E.F. wrote Commanding General, 40th Division "The Commander-in-Chief directs that you furnish, with the least practicable delay, to the Commanding General, S.O.S., a sample of the distinctive insignia authorized for your command with complete description and dimensions." On 2 March 1919 by 1st Ind. Det. Hq. 40th Div., A.E.F. wrote to Comdg. General, S.O.S., A.E.F. "1. Patch blue cloth three inches square in center of which is embroidered in yellow silk representation of the sun, consisting of centre 13 – 16 inches in diameter with twelve rays approximately 3- 16 inches wide at base and 1-2 inch long. To be worn with one corner of patch up. 2. Sample inclosed."

On 31 March 1922, a memorandum from War Department General Staff to the Adjutant General of the Army noted that "1. The present 40th Division is the successor of the former 40th Division and as such is authorized to wear the blue square and yellow sun insignia. ..." and "2. The shoulder patch of the 40th Division is described as follows: On a blue square 2 1/2" on a side a sun in splendor in yellow, the disc 13/16" in diameter with 12 rays whose points lie within a circle 1 7/8" in diameter."

Symbolism: The design alludes to California, where the division had its origin, while the blue field alludes to the sky and the Pacific Ocean.

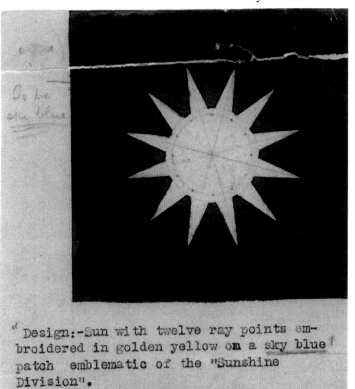

Design drawing inclosed with 17 November 1918 communication of G.G., 40th Division to C in C, A.E.F.

FORTY-FIRST DIVISION
LINEAGE

Constituted 18 July 1917 in the National Guard as Headquarters, 41st Division. Organized 18 September 1917 at Camp Greene, North Carolina with troops from the western states and District of Columbia. Demobilized 22 February 1919 at Camp Dix, New Jersey. (41st Division formerly 20th Division.)

CAMPAIGN PARTICIPATION

World War I

Streamer without inscription

Approved: 28 December 1918

On or before 25 December 1918 Commanding General, 41st Division wrote Commanding General, S.O.S. requesting authority for a distinctive shoulder insignia. By telegram of 25 December Commanding General S.O.S. wrote C IN C HAEF "1570-G-1 PERIOD COMMANDING GENERAL FORTY FIRST DIVISION HAS REQUESTED AUTHORITY TO DESIGNATE SHOULDER INSIGNIA FOR THAT DIVISION PERIOD IT IS RECOMMENTED THAT THIS DIVISION BE ASSIGNED SUITABLE SHOULDER INSIGNIA PERIOD". In reply of same date G.H.Q., A.E.F. by telegram advised Commanding General, S.O.S. "M-1107 Reference your telegram 1570 G-1. Authority is granted for distinctive shoulder insignia for 41st Division. Submit sample for approval with least practicable delay." On 26 December Commanding General, Services of Supply wrote Commander-in-Chief, G.1 "1. In accordance with wire from your headquarters approving shoulder insignia for the 41st Division, the enclosed design is submitted for approval. 2. Since this division is moving out within a short time it is requested that, if satisfactory, approval of this insignia be wired to these headquarters as soon as possible." On 28 December 1918 G.H.Q., A.E.F. to Commanding General, S.O.S. telegrammed "M-1147. Distinctive insignia for 41st Division comma as submitted with your letter of December 26, 1918 comma is approved period".

On February 18, 1919, Commanding General, 41st Division then headquartered at Camp Dix, New Jersey, wrote to The Adjutant General of the Army "1. Relative to your communication of January 7th 1919 to Commanding General, 41st Division as to distinctive name or divisional design adopted by this division. I am forwarding inclosed shoulder shield representing a sunset, the division being known as the "Sunset Division", on account of most of troops of original division being from the Northwest. 2. This design was approved by the Commanding General, S.O.S., American E.F., December 30th 1918." (Note: O.Q.M.G. sheet 5-2-7 confirms approval date of CG AEF as 28 December 1918.)

On 21 June 1922, a memorandum from War Department General Staff to the Adjutant General of the Army stated "The Secretary of War directs that the drawing herewith be sent to the Quartermaster General, together with a communication in substance as follows: The shoulder sleeve insignia of the 41st Division was approved by telegram, December 28, 1918 from the Adjutant General, A. E. F. to the Commanding General, 41st Division. It is described as follows: On a red semi disc 2 – 1/2" in diameter a blue base line 1/8" in width and the setting sun in yellow. The demi sun of 12 rays, root circle 3/4" radius, point circle 1 – 1/8" radius."

Symbolism: The division was organized with personnel from National Guard units from several western states, and the design alludes to the setting sun over the Pacific Ocean.

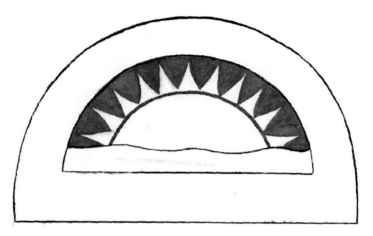

Design drawing inclosed with 26 December 1918 communication of Commanding General, Services of Supply to Commander-in-Chief, G.1.

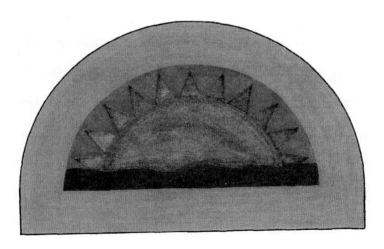

Design painting from the records of the National Archives.

FORTY-SECOND DIVISION
LINEAGE
Constituted 14 August 1917 in the National Guard as Headquarters, 42nd Division. Organized 5 September 1917 at Camp Mills, New York with troops from New York. Demobilized 9 May 1919 at Camp Dix, New Jersey.
CAMPAIGN PARTICIPATION
World War I
Champagne-Marne
Aisne-Marne
St. Mihiel
Meuse-Argonne
Champaign 1918
Lorraine 1919
Approved: 29 October 1918

On 20 October 1918 Commanding General, 42d Division wrote to Commanding General, Fifth Army Corps "1. It is recommended that the shoulder insignia for the 42d Division be of one of the designs shown in attached drawing. 2. If colors are to be permitted in the design the quarter circle rainbow in blue, yellow and red is suggested. If only one color is to be used then the semi-circle band indicating the shape of a rainbow is suggested. A light colored khaki insignia would appear well on the background of the olive drab woolen coat and overcoat as issued." By 1st Ind on 22 October the letter was forwarded to the Commanding General, First Army. On same date HQRS 42ND DIVN wrote ADJT GENL HAEF by telegram "A G EIGHT ELEVEN PERIOD RETEL M DASH SIX SEVEN FOUR DESIGN FOR DIVN WILL BE ONE INCH QUARTER CIRCLE BAND OF WHICH RADIUS OF OUTER EDGE ONE AND THREE QUARTERS INCH PERIOD THIS BAND COMPOSED OF THREE COLORED BAND EACH ONE THIRD INCH WIDE COLORS BLUE YELLOW AND RED THE LATTER BEING OUTSIDE COLOR PERIOD CAN ARRANGE PURCHASE SAME WHEN DESIGN IS APPROVED". In reply by telegram of same date from G.H.Q., A.E.F. to Commanding General, 42d Division wrote "Number M-712. Reference you telegram A G eight eleven comma submit by mail sample or drawing of selected period Upon receipt of this comma decision as to approval will be made." On 26 October 1918, by letter the design was forwarded to G.H.Q., A.E.F. which replied by telegram to Commanding General, 42d Division on 29 October 1918 "Number M-759. Reference your letter of October twenty-six comma design adopted as insignia for 42d Division is approved." On 15 November 1918 Commanding General, 42nd Division wrote to Commanding General, First Army "1. Pursuant to telegraphic instructions from the Adjutant General, A.E.F., October 19, 1918, the following described insignia was adopted and telegraphic description forwarded to General Headquarters followed by color drawing: "design for division will be one inch quarter circle band of which radius of outer edge is one and three-quarter inches, this band composed of three colored bands each one-third inch wide, colors blue, yellow and red, the latter being outside color." 2. This design was approved by General Headquarters by telegram dated October 29, 1918 (M 759)."
On 26 May 1922, a memorandum from War Department General Staff to the Adjutant General of the Army stated "The Secretary of War directs that the drawing herewith be sent

to the Quartermaster General, together with a communication in substance as follows: The shoulder sleeve insignia of the 42nd Division is described as follows: The 4th quadrant of a rainbow of three bands red, yellow and blue, 2" radius, each 3/8" in width."

Symbolism: The 42[d] Division is known as the "Rainbow Division" because personnel from 26 states originally formed the division.

The following background and description of the SHOULDER INSIGNIA OF THE 42ND DIVISION was observed in the records of The Institute of Heraldry:

"1. The shoulder insignia of the 42nd Division is a Rainbow. It was approved by G.H.Q. October 29, 1918 and was first officially worn December 4, 1918 at Welschbillig, Germany. 2. The insignia was designed by Colonel William N. Hughes, Jr., Chief of Staff, 42nd Division. 3. The insignia is a parti-colored quadrant, suggesting, in conventional design, the arc of a rainbow (sketch attached). The Division was known, even before its organization, as the Rainbow Division and was so referred to in the American Press prior to the decision of the War Department to make the first National Guard Division for service in France a representative American Division by combining in its composition units from the National Guard organizations of as many states as possible. As a consequence, the Division contains organizations from the following states, representing every section of the United States except New England:

Louisiana	Kansas
Pennsylvania	Texas
New York	North Carolina
Ohio	New Jersey
Wisconsin	Tennessee
Alabama	Oklahoma
Iowa	Michigan
Georgia	District of Columbia
Illinois	Nebraska
Indiana	Oregon
Minnesota	Colorado
Maryland	Missouri
South Carolina	California
Virginia	

4. The name "Rainbow Division" was cordially accepted by the Division as soon as formed, and it has borne it ever since. The record of the Division in war is second to none in the American Army; its name has become a household word at home and the selection of the Rainbow has proved a most happy one on many occasions, in the inspiration that has been given to the Division in several engagements by the appearance of an actual Rainbow in the sky as it was going into action. It would almost seem that the Rainbow has adopted the Division, even as the Division has adopted the Rainbow."

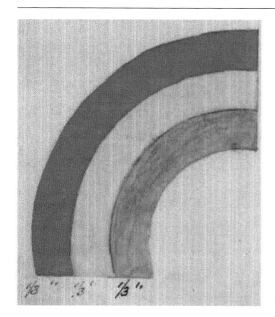

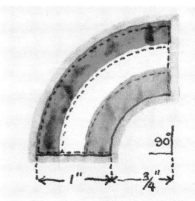

DESIGN FOR CHEVRON
FOR RAINBOW DIVISION
TO BE MADE OF THREE
STRIPS - RED, YELLOW
AND BLUE - EACH STRIP
⅓" WIDE, STITCHED TO
OLIVE DRAB

Drawing believed to have accompanied 20 October 1918 communication of Commanding General, 42d Division to Commanding General, Fifth Army Corps.

Design drawing inclosed with 26 October 1918 communication referenced in 29 October 1918 telegram M-759 of G.H.Q., A.E.F. to Commanding General, 42d Division.

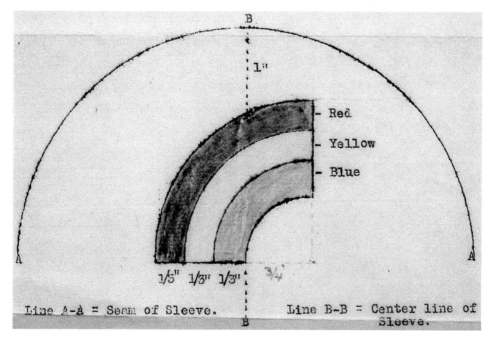

Drawing depicted on 4 December 1918 Memorandum No. 328 of Headquarters 42nd Division illustrating how the Divisional insignia is to be worn.

SEVENTY-SIXTH DIVISION
LINEAGE
Constituted 5 August 1917 in the National Army as Headquarters, 76th Division. Organized 25 August 1917 at Camp Devens, Massachusetts. Demobilized 14 January 1919 at Camp Devens, Massachusetts.
CAMPAIGN PARTICIPATION
World War I
Streamer without inscription
Approved: 14 March 1919

On 7 March 1919 Lt. Col. G. M. Peek, G. S., VII Army Corps wrote to the Adjutant General, G.H.Q. "1. Having been Chief of Staff of the 76th Division from shortly after its arrival overseas until same was skeletonized, I have been requested to furnish information regarding the arm insignia of that division. 2. The arm insignia which was tentatively adopted by the 76th Division is inclosed herewith and marked "Exhibit A", but due to the division being skeletonized and returned to the United States no formal application was ever made for its approval. I find that there are a few men, formerly members of the 76th Division, wearing an insignia of the design inclosed herewith and marked "Exhibit B", claiming it to be the insignia assigned the 76th Division by G.H.Q. Information is requested as to whether or not the records show such an insignia to have been assigned to this division. If such is not the case, it is requested that the insignia inclosed herewith and marked "Exhibit A" be recorded as the official insignia of the 76th Division. This insignia is the shield upon which the official crest of the division was made up and was used to mark baggage and transportation both in the United States and France." By 1st Ind. of March 14, 1919 G. H. Q., American E. F. replied "Exhibit A is made of record as the distinctive insignia of the 76th Division."

On 21 June 1922, a memorandum from War Department General Staff to the Adjutant General of the Army stated "The Secretary of War directs that the drawing herewith be sent to the Quartermaster General, together with a communication in substance as follows: The shoulder sleeve insignia of the 76th Division was approved by telegram March 14, 1919 from the Adjutant General, A. E. F. to the Commanding General, 76th Division. It is described as follows: An "eared" shield 2 – 1/4" in height and 1-3/4" in width, whose edges are straight lines, red, a blue chief separated by an olive drab line 1/8" in width. The chief charged with a white label with dovetailed points."

Symbolism: Red, white, and blue are the national colors, while the label, a symbol of cadency, denotes that the division was one of the first National Army divisions.

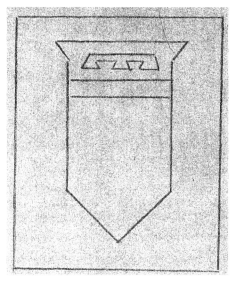

Design drawing from the records of the
National Archives.

Design painting from the records of the National Archives.

SEVENTY-SEVENTH DIVISION
LINEAGE
Constituted 5 August 1917 in the National Army as Headquarters, 77th Division. Organized 18 August 1917 at Camp Upton, New York. Demobilized 9 May 1919 at Camp Upton, New York.
CAMPAIGN PARTICIPATION
World War I
Oise-Aisne
Meuse-Argonne
Champaign 1918
Approved: 23 October 1918

On 22 October 1918 by telegram G 1 77th DIVN wrote to THE ADJT GENERAL GHQ AEF "NUMBER ONE G TWO THREE SEVEN PERIOD IN REPLY TO YOUR M SIX SEVEN FOUR THE DISTINCTIVE CLOTH DESIGN ADOPTED BY THE SEVENTY SEVENTH DIVISION IS AS FOLLOWS COLON LIBERTY STATUE TWO AND ONE QUARTER INCHES HIGH IN GOLD ON BLUE BACKGROUND TWO AND ONE HALF INCHES HIGH WIDTH AT TOP ONE INCH AT BOTTOM TWO INCHES PERIOD FIGURE TO BE CUT FROM GOLD CLOTH AND APPLIED ON BLUE BACKGROUND". On same date G.H.Q., A.E.F. replied by telegram to Commanding General, 77th Division "Number M-715. Reference your telegram Number one G two three seven comma design adopted by Seventy-seventh Division is approved period Submit by mail sample of design or drawing and complete description thereof for records of these Headquarters." On 24 October 1918 Commanding General, 77th Division wrote The Adjutant General, G.H.Q., American E.F. "1. In compliance with your telegram M-715, the following description of design adopted by 77th Division is submitted and drawing enclosed. 2. This design will consist of blue field, 2 1/2 inches high with 2 inch base and measuring one (1) inch at the top, with a gold Statue of Liberty 2 1/4 inches high thereon. This figure to be either cut from yellow cloth and applied to blue field or it may be embroidered in gold."

On 26 May 1922, a memorandum from War Department General Staff to the Adjutant General of the Army stated "The Secretary of War directs that the drawing herewith be sent to the Quartermaster General, together with a communication in substance as follows: The shoulder sleeve insignia of the 77th Division is described as follows: On a blue truncated pyramid 2 3/4" in height, 2" in width at base, 1" in width at top the Statue of Liberty without masonry base, in New York Harbor, in yellow."

Symbolism: The Statue of Liberty design alludes to New York City, where
the division was raised.

Preliminary design drawing from the records of the National Archives.

Drawing inclosed with 24 October 1918 communication of Commanding General, 77th Division to the Adjutant General, G.H.Q., A.E.F.

Design painting from the records of the National Archives.

SEVENTY-EIGHTH DIVISION
LINEAGE

Constituted 5 August 1917 in the National Army as Headquarters, 78th Division. Organized 23 August 1917 at Camp Dix, New Jersey. Demobilized 9 July 1919 at Camp Dix, New Jersey.

CAMPAIGN PARTICIPATION

World War I

St. Mihiel

Meuse-Argonne

Lorraine 1918

Approved: 20 October 1918, 24 January 1919 and 8 March 1919

On 19 October 1918 by telegram from Commanding General, 78th Division, to ADJ. GENL HAEF wrote "FOUR NINE FOUR G DASH ONE PERIOD RETEL NUMBER M 574 DESIGN ADOPTED RED SEMICIRCLE THREE INCHES IN DIAMETER TO BE WORN CIRCUMFERENCE ON TOP". (It appears that the reference to telegram M-574 was in error and should have been M-674. In reply on 20 October 1918 G.H.Q., A.E.F. by telegram to Commanding General, 78th Division advised "M-683. Reference your telegram of October nineteenth the design of red semicircle adopted by seventy-eighth Division is approved." Also on 19 October another telegram was sent from 78th Division to Adjutant General, HAEF as follows "One nine naught naught period Retel M six seven four advise that this Division has adopted subject to approval the design of a half circle of red flannel three inches in diameter". A notation on the copy indicates the telegram was received "A.G.O. 22 OCT 1918 G.H.Q., A.E.F.", and thus two days after the approval telegram M-683 of 20 October 1918.

There is some conflicting information on the appropriate date of the approval, however, the copy of telegram M-683 of G.H.Q., A.E.F. of 20 October 1918 clarifies that date as being the verified approval date. (On O.Q.M.G. sheet 5-2-8 the approval is listed as CG. AEF. Oct 29, 1918 & Jan. 24, 1919. However, on 24 October 1918 the memorandum from General Headquarters, American Expeditionary Forces setting forth "...the divisions which have submitted descriptions of the distinctive insignia adopted, and which have been approved by this office,..." described the design as: "Red semicircle, 3 in. in diameter, to be worn circumference on top.")

On January 24, 1919, Headquarters, 78th Division by telegram to Adjutant General, Haef wrote "919 G one period Request authority to change shoulder insignia this division by addition of white streak of lightning across the red semicircle period The lightning division name is thus more clearly indicated period Request early reply." On same date G.H.Q., A.E.F. replied "M-188 Reference your 919 G one Authority is granted to change present shoulder insignia by addition of white streak lightning thru red semicircle".

Subsequently, on 20 February 1919 The Division Commander, 78th Division wrote to Commander-in-Chief, General Headquarters, American E.F., in which he expressed concern the Chief Quartermaster, Paris had cancelled the order for the insignia on the direction of G.H.Q., and that there was a misunderstanding regarding the cost and the addition of the approved lightning streak. By 2nd Ind. on 3 March Commanding General, 78th Division to Commander-in-Chief, American E.F. wrote "1. Request reconsideration of revocation of telegram authorizing the addition of a streak of lightning to the emblem of this Division. It is believed this revocation is based on a misconception of the facts. All that is desired is simply add a streak of lightning to the sleeve insignia. Very little expense will be entailed. We prefer to have a streak of lightning embroidered with white silver threads, but if this is too expensive a white felt patch cut out by a stencil, and sewed on would be satisfactory. 2. The name "Lightning Division" was given to this division as a result of a popular vote at Camp Dix. The Divisional design has always had a representation of lightning placed on it. It is very desirable that the sleeve insignia and the regular divisional design should agree." By 3rd Ind. on 8 March 1919 G.H.Q., A.E.F. advised Commanding General, 78th Division "The addition of a streak of lightning to the insignia of the 78th Division is authorized, provided no additional expense to the Government is entailed therein."

On 26 May 1922, a memorandum from War Department General Staff to the Adjutant General of the Army stated "The Secretary of War directs that the drawing herewith be sent to the Quartermaster General, together with a communication in substance as follows: The shoulder sleeve insignia of the 78th Division is described as follows: On a red semi-disc 3" in diameter a white lightning bolt from sinister chief to dexter base."

Symbolism: The lightning flash on the red background alludes to the combat record of the division likened to a "bolt of lightning ...." And to its designation as the "Lightning Division."

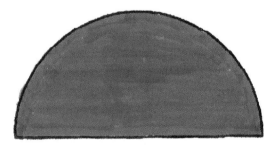

Sketch based on description as approved 19 October 1918.

Design drawing depicting addition of the lightning streak proposed
in 24 January 1919 telegram 919 G 1 and approved by G.H.Q.,
A.E.F. telegram M-188.

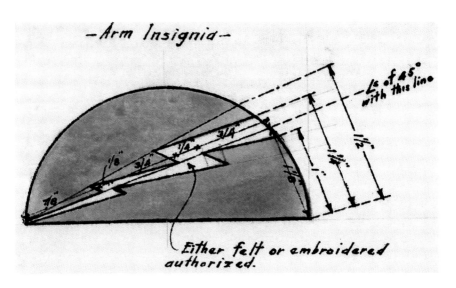

Design painting in the records of the National Archives depicting design details.

SEVENTY-NINTH DIVISION

LINEAGE

Constituted 5 August 1917 in the National Army as Headquarters, 79th Division. Organized 25 August 1917 at Camp Meade, Maryland. Demobilized 2 June 1919 at Camp Dix, New Jersey.

CAMPAIGN PARTICIPATION

World War I

Meuse-Argonne

Lorraine 1918

Approved: 16 November 1918

On 20 October 1918 Commanding General, 79th division by telegram wrote ADJUTANT GENERAL, GHQAEF "A G NO 492 PERIOD REFERENCE TELEGRAM M FIVE SEVEN FOUR PERIOD FOLLOWING DESIGN SELECTED FOR SEVENTY NINTH DIVISION COLON FIVE POINTED STAR INSCRIBED IN CIRCLE THREE AND THREE FOURTHS INCHES IN DIAMETER COMMA REENTRANT BETWEEN POINTS OF STAR TANGENT TO INTERIOR CIRCLE ONE AND SEVEN EIGHTS INCHES IN DIAMETER SEMICOLON CHRIMSON WOOLEN CLOTH COMMA SEWED ON LEFT SLEEVE WITH ONE POINT OF STAR TANGENT TO SHOULDER SEAM AND CENTER OF LOWER END OF SHOULDER STRAP PERIOD PLEASE ADVISE IF APPROVED". In reply, on 21 October G.H.Q., A.E.F. advised Commanding General, 79th Division by telegram "Number M-692. Reference you A G 492 comma submit drawing or sample of design to this office without delay period Upon receipt of this comma decision as to approval will be wired you." On 23 October Commanding General, 79th Division replied by letter to Adjutant General, A. E. F. "1. In compliance with telegram instructions of October 21, 1918, M 692, two drawings and designs of the proposed insignia of the 79th Division are submitted herewith for approval. 2. If approved, telegraphic authority is requested so that prompt action may be taken to secure same." On 6 November 1918 G.H.Q., A.E.F. replied by telegram to Commanding General, 79th Division "Number M-811. Reference your letter of October twenty-third comma design submitted as insignia for 79th Division cannot be approved on account of similarity to approved design of 2d Division Period Another design will be selected and reported by wire to this office for consideration comma sample or drawing with complete description thereof to be sent by mail for records of these Headquarters."

On 13 November 1918 Commanding General, 79th Division wrote Adjutant General, American E.F. "Confirming our telegram on the above subject, copy enclosed, there are enclosed herewith three designs of insignia of 79th Division. Our selection and preference is in the following order: 1st – STAR IN CIRCLE ON BLACK FIELD: This design is preferred as it has been the design which the Division adopted prior to leaving Camp Meade, Md., and with which officers' baggage was at that time marked, and it has identified the Division ever since its arrival in France. 2nd – ORANGE STAR ON BLACK KEYSTONE: The Keystone is represented by Pennsylvania troops, the Star by Washington, D.C., Orange and Black being the colors of Maryland. The troops of this Division are from Washington, Maryland and Eastern Pennsylvania. 3rd – GRAY LORRAINE CROSS ON BLUE SHIELD: This is selected because of its simplicity and being easy to paint on trucks as well as having a distinct significance. 4th - LIBERTY BELL: (Design not submitted.)" By telegram on 14 November G.H.Q., A.E.F. advised Commanding General, 79th division "M-855. Reference your telegram AG 810 submit by mail samples or drawings of first and third designs period Second not available." (Reference to telegram AG 810 of 79th Division is believed in error.) By telegram of 16 November 1918 G.H.Q., A.E.F. to Commanding General, 79th Division advised "Number M-865. Reference your letter of November thirteenth comma impossible to approve first or second design submitted on account of similarity to approved designs of other Divisions period third design submitted comma Gray Lorraine Cross on blue shield comma is approved as distinctive design for Seventy-ninth Division."

In ORDERS No. 72 of HEADQUARTERS, 79th DIVISION on 20 December 1918 the specifications of the Lorraine Cross design were "To be made of two patches, centered, (b) sewed on (a): (a) Base patch: Gray – a shield 2 1-2" wide at top and 2 5-8" high. (b) Cut-out patch: Blue – a shield 2 3-8" wide at top and 2 1-2" high, and enclosing a cut-out Lorraine cross 2 3-8" high, with arms 1-4" thick and 1 3-8" and 1 1-2" long."

On O.Q.M.G. sheet 5-2-8 approval is noted as AG, AEF. Nov. 16, 1918. In ORDERS No. 24 of 22nd January 1919 HEADQUARTERS, 79th DIVISION, AMERICAN E. F. wrote "VII. HISTORY OF DIVISION INSIGNIA. The Lorraine Cross is the symbol of Triumph. Since the great battle of Nancy in the 15th Century when the defeat of Charles the Bold, Duke of Burgundy, ushered in the glorious reign of the House of Anjou, (Rene II, 1473 – 1508), the Cross was adopted as the sign of victory of the reigning house. Not only to the people of the Province of Lorraine but to the French nation the triumph of justice and right in the historical battle remains one of their most popular national souvenirs, and the Lorraine Cross is but the outward symbol wherein is centered the affectionate and zealous love of a nation for liberty, justice and freedom."

On 21 June 1922, a memorandum from War Department General Staff to the Adjutant General of the Army stated "The Secretary of War directs that the drawing herewith be sent to the Quartermaster General, together with a communication in substance as follows: The shoulder sleeve insignia of the 79th Division was approved by telegram November 16, 1918 from the Adjutant General, A. E. F. to the Commanding General, 79th Division. It is described as follows: A blue triangular shield 2 1/2" in height by 2 1/8" in width, a Lorraine Cross within an orle. Cross and orle silver gray and the elements of each 1/8" in width."

Symbolism: The cross symbolizes triumph and alludes to service in the Lorraine
                      area of France.

Design drawing submitted with 13 November 1918 communication of Commanding General, 79th Division to Adjutant General, American E.F. and approved by telegram M-865 of 16 November 1918. (Drawing was in color as pictured.)

Design drawing in color submitted with 13 November 1918 communication of Commanding General, 79th Division to Adjutant General, American E.F. and approved by telegram M-865 of 16 November 1918.

Design painting from the records of the National Archives.

EIGHTIETH DIVISION
LINEAGE
Constituted 5 August 1917 in the National Army as Headquarters, 80ᵗʰ Division. Organized 27 August 1917 at Camp Lee, Virginia. Demobilized 5 June 1919 at Camp Lee, Virginia.
CAMPAIGN PARTICIPATION
World War I
    Somme Offensive
    Meuse-Argonne
Approved: 20 October 1918

On 19 October 1918 Commanding General, 80ᵗʰ Division by telegram to THE ADJUTANT GENERAL, HAEF wrote "NO.M. SIX SEVEN FOUR REPORT DESIGN FORE EIGHTH-BLUE RIDGE, DIVISION SHIELD TWO AND ONE FOURTH INCHES BROAD AND DEEP MADE OF OLIVE DRAB CLOTH AND BEARING SUPERIMPOSED IN CENTER THREE BLUE HILLS THREE FOURTH INCHES HIGH ALL OUTLINED IN WHITE AND SYMBOLICAL OF STATES OF VIRGINIA WEST VIRGINIA AND PENNSYLVANIA". By telegram of 20 October G.H.Q., A.E.F. to Commanding General, 80ᵗʰ Division advised: "M-686. Reference your telegram of October nineteenth the design adopted by Eightieth Division is approved."

By 1ˢᵗ Ind. of 23 February 1919 Hq. 80ᵗʰ Div., A.E.F. to Commanding General, S.O.S., American Expeditionary Forces wrote "1. Forwarded, enclosing sample of distinctive insignia worn on the left sleeve at the shoulder by members of the 80ᵗʰ Division. 2. The shield is two inches square, outlined in white on a khaki patch. In the middle of the shield are superimposed three blue hills, representing the Blue Ridge Mountains which extend through the three States from which the members of this Division were called to the service, namely: Pennsylvania, West Virginia, and Virginia."

On 21 June 1922, a memorandum from War Department General Staff to the Adjutant General of the Army stated "The Secretary of War directs that the drawing herewith be sent to the Quartermaster General, together with a communication in substance as follows: The shoulder sleeve insignia of the 80th Division was approved by telegram October 20, 1918 from the Adjutant General, A. E. F. to the Commanding General, 80th Division. It is described as follows: An "eared" shield 2 1/4" in height by 1 3/4" in width, bottom of shield a double ogee in outline. Olive drab within a narrow border of white three blue mountains. Base of maintains separated from base of shield by a white line. Width of line and width of border 1/8"."

Symbolism: The three blue stylized mountains, one for each state, allude to the "Blue Ridge" states (Pennsylvania, Virginia, and West Virginia), from which personnel of the division originally came.

Drawing inclosed with 23 October 1918 communication of Commanding General, 80th Division to The Adjutant General, G.H.Q, American E.F.

Design painting from the records of The Institute of Heraldry.

EIGHTY-FIRST DIVISION
LINEAGE
Constituted 5 August 1917 in the National Army as Headquarters, 81st Division. Organized 25 August 1917 at Camp Jackson, South Carolina. Demobilized 11 June 1919 at Hoboken, New Jersey.
CAMPAIGN PARTICIPATION
World War I
    Meuse-Argonne
    Lorraine 1918
Approved: 19 October 1918

On 28 September 1918 the Adjutant General, G.H.Q., A.E.F. wrote to Commanding General, 81st Division requesting that authority be furnished, if any, for wearing the "wildcat" in cloth on both the left sleeve and the overseas cap. In reply by 1st Ind. on 4 October 1918 Commanding General, 81st Division, Major General Charles J. Bailey to the Commander in Chief, A.E.F. wrote "1. There is no official sanction for wearing the above mentioned emblem. 2. The following is submitted with the request that it receive carefully consideration before definite action is taken. 3. In making an inspection of the various fronts last winter, I observed that several British Divisions wore a distinctive emblem on the shoulder, or middle of the back, and that all the divisions I saw, British and French, had some distinctive silhouette on trucks, wagons and certain equipment. I was informed by the British that this emblem worn by the men did much to develop Divisional espirit; that the men were proud of it and that it was particularly valuable in an active operation in identifying and controlling the smaller units. 4. On returning to the States, I found that the War Department had authorized the Divisions to adapt distinctive names and also insignia for identifying its trains etc. As this Division was, and is, about 95% Southern in its personnel, and was organized at Camp Jackson, S. C. the name adopted was The "Stonewall" Division after General "Stonewall" Jackson. Camp Jackson is situated on Wildcat Creek and a Wildcat was adopted as the insignia of the Division, and all transportation, boxes, field desks etc., were so marked and its number, 81, omitted. 5. Placing a small silhouette on the left shoulder of officers and men and on the overseas cap of the officers, has resulted as follows: (a) It has created a comradeship in the personnel by keeping in evidence the sections whence it came - all the Southern States around the South Carolina. These men came mostly from the mountains and other agricultural and sparsely settled communities. They are unused to large crowds; are shy with strangers and we're very slow in "getting together". A common interest, social in a way, one that would promote good fellowship, aside from military team work, was developed at once and the insignia brings individuals together who would not otherwise know or care for one another. (b.) Much more important, the insignia has developed a divisional espirit which is most satisfactory. I do not, and cannot claim that this division is superior to the next one but I claim that any measure I can take will lead the personnel to think their own the best, makes for efficiency and progress. The pride the men take in the insignia is shown in their conduct, their efficiency and their evident belief that they are as good as any, and perhaps a little better. I cannot say they are better than the other divisions, now at the front, or showing themselves to be, but it is certain that the espirit developed by the measure now in question has not only bettered the individual, but has made the task of training, developing the fighting spirit, and teamwork, much easier than was thought possible with men whose former environment had not only developed independence of thought and action, but have also rendered them impatient of restraint and slow to give obedience. (c.) An insignia of some nature would seem of considerable advantage in handling small units in the present methods of advance in open warfare. 6. Beyond the foregoing, the only reason I would advance for adopting the insignia is that it seemed to be carrying out the spirit of the instructions permitting distinctive working of organizations rather than numbers heretofore displayed on personnel and material. 7. I have been confirmed in the correctness of my opinion by the fact that many American, French and British officers have volunteered to me their approval of the use of the insignia, and noe have criticized it."

Subsequently, General Bailey met with General Pershing, and after reconsideration G.H.Q., A.E.F. on 18 October 1918 issued telegram "NUMBER M-674 EACH DIVISION WILL ADOPT AND PROCURE IMMEDIATELY SOME DISTINCTIVE CLOTH DESIGN WHICH WILL BE WORN BY EVERY OFFICER AND MAN OF THE DIVISION ON THE LEFT ARM COMMA, THE UPPER PART TO BE ATTACHED TO THE SHOULDER SEAM PERIOD REPORT WILL BE MADE TO THESE HEADQUARTERS BY TELEGRAM AS TO DESIGNS ADOPTED IN ORDER THAT THERE MAY BE NO DUPLICATION APPROVAL OF DESIGN WILL BE MADE BY TELEGRAM FROM THESE HEADQUARTERS." On same date Commanding General, 81st Division, by telegram wrote Adjutant General, AEF, GHQ "REFERENCE TELEGRAM M SIX SEVEN FOUR OCTOBER EIGHTEEN DAVIS COMMA EIGHTY FIRST DIVISION ADOPTED WILD CAT AS INSIGNIA IN DIVISION GENERAL ORDERS SIXTEEN MAY TWENTY FOURTH PERIOD REQUEST CONFIRMATION". By telegram of 19 October 1918 G.H.Q., A.E.F. replied to Commanding General, 81st Division, "Number M-681. Reference your telegram of October nineteenth comma the adoption of wild cat as insignia for Eighty-first Division is approved." On 22 October 1918 by telegram to Commanding General, 81st Division, G.H.Q., A.E.F. advised "Number M-710. Reference your telegram October nineteenth relative Division insignia comma submit to this office by mail without delay sample of design adopted or drawing and complete description thereof for records these Headquarters." By letter of 23 October the Commanding General, 81st Division wrote The Adjutant General, General Headquarters "1. In compliance with your telegram number M-10, 22nd October, 1918, enclose the following: (a) Drawing of the division insignia, as it appears on property of the division. (b) Drawing of the division insignia, as it appears in the form of a chevron worn by every officer and man of the division on the left upper arm. Different colored cats indicate different branches of the service, as outlined in G.O. #16, May 24th, 1918, these Headquarters. (It will be noted that the letters "C", "O" and "L" do not appear on the chevron.) (c) G.O. #16, Hqrs., 81st Division, May 24th, 1918, announcing the wildcat as the unofficial division insignia and prescribing its use."

GENERAL ORDERS No. 16 issued by HEADQUARTERS 81ST DIVISION on 24 May 1918 is as follows:

"1. The 81st Division will be known hereafter unofficially as the STONEWALL DIVISION. The motto of the Division will be "OBEDIENCE, COURAGE, LOYALTY". The unofficial insignia of the Division will be a wildcat with the letters "O" on the left, "C" above, and "L" on the right. The insignia will be stenciled on division vehicles and other property, the pattern to be furnished by these Headquarters and to be followed exactly. 2. In applying the stencil, the following colors will be used:

Division Headquarters and Headquarters Troop: black cat, black letters.

156th Artillery Brigade: red cat throughout the brigade.

     Brigade Headquarters: red letters

316th Regiment: red O, Black C, black L.

317th Regiment: black O, red C, black L.

318th Regiment: black O, black C, red L.

161 Infantry Brigade: white cat throughout the brigade.

     Brigade Headquarters: red letters.

321st Regiment: red O, black C, black L.

322nd Regiment: black O, red C, black L.

317th Machine Gun Bn.: black O, black C, red L.

162nd Infantry Brigade: sky blue cat throughout the brigade.

     Brigade Headquarters: red letters.

323rd Regiment: red O, black C, black L.

324th Regiment: black O, red C, black L.

318th Machine Gun Battn.: Black O, black O, red L.

306th Regiment Engineers: black cat throughout, red letters.

306th Field Signal Battalion: orange cat, black letters.

306th Train Hq. and Military Police: black cat, sky blue letters.

306th Sanitary Train: green cat, black letters.

306th Supply Train: yellow cat, black letters.

306th Trench Mortar Battery: red cat, dark blue letters.

316th Machine Gun Battalion: black cat white letters.

Regiments will designate the first battalion by a red bar beneath the device, the second battalion by a white bar, and the third battalion by a sky blue bar. Trains will use a similar designation for sections."

On 24 October 1918, the memorandum from General Headquarters American Expeditionary Forces setting forth "…the divisions which have submitted descriptions of the distinctive insignia adopted, and which have been approved by this office,…" described the design as "Wild cat."

On 30 January 1919, on a 1st Ind. from Hq. 81st Division, American E. F. France Commanding General, C. J. Bailey wrote to The Adjutant General of the Army:

"1. The name "Stonewall Division" and the insignia a Wildcat were adopted by this Division at Camp Sevier, S. C., May 24, 1918, and announced in Paragraphs 1 and 2, General Orders No. 16, these headquarters. Copies inclosed. 2. Samples of Division sleeve insignia are enclosed herewith as follows:

Div. Hqs. Div. M. G. Bn., and Engineer Regiment	Black
161st Infantry Brigade	White
162nd Infantry Brigade	Light Blue
156th Field Artillery Brigade & Ammunition Train	Red
306th Field signal Battalion	Orange
306th Sanitary Train	Green
306th Supply Train	Buff"

(Note that the color yellow for the cat as cited in G.O. No. 16 for the 306th Supply Train was substituted as buff in the aforesaid communications.)

On 21 February 1919 Commanding General, 81st Division wrote Commanding General, S. O. S., American E. F.:

1. In compliance with letter from Adjutant General, G.H.Q., of February 19th, you are informed that the enclosed shoulder insignia is the one adopted by the 81st Division. 2. The various units of the Division have different colored insignia, as follows:

Division. Hdqrs. and Hdqrs, Troop	Black
161st Infantry Brigade	White
162nd Infantry Brigade	Blue
306th Sanitary Train	Green
306th Field Signal Battalion	Orange
306th Supply Train	Buff
156th Artillery Brigade	Red
306th Ammunition Train	Red
306th Engrs. and Train	Black
316th Machine Gun Battalion	Black"

On the "FILE COPY" A.G.O. S.O.S. Record 305-2 is the notation written "Approved 10/19/18".

On 27 June 1922, a memorandum from War Department General Staff to the Adjutant General of the Army stated "The Secretary of War directs that the drawing herewith be sent to the Quartermaster General, together with a communication in substance as follows: The shoulder sleeve insignia of the 81st Division was approved by telegram October 19, 1918 from the Adjutant General, A. E. F. to the Commanding General, 81st Division. It is described as follows: On an olive drab disc 2 inches in diameter within a black circle 1/8" in width a black wild cat passant."

Symbolism: The wildcat is common to the Carolinas, from which many of the original personnel of the division came. Also the division trained at Camp Jackson, South Carolina, along Wild Cat Creek

Design drawing (reduced) enclosed with 23 October 1918 communication of Commanding General, 81st Division to The Adjutant General, General Headquarters depicting insignia pursuant to G.O. #16 24 May 1918. Note the sample design of the shoulder insignia in the upper left corner.

Division Headquarters and Headquarters Troop, 316th Machine Gun Battalion, and 306th Engineer Regiment and Train (Black wildcat and border). Design painting from the records of The Institute of Heraldry.

161st Infantry Brigade (White wildcat and border). Sample from the collection of The Johnson Brothers.

162nd Infantry Brigade (Blue wildcat and border). Design painting from records of The Institutue of Heraldry.

156th Artillery Brigade and Ammunition Train (Red wildcat and border). Design painting from the records of the National Archives.

306th Field Signal Battalion (Orange wildcat and border). Design painting from the records of The Institute of Heraldry.

306th Sanitary Train (Green wildcat and border). Sketch based on description.

306th Supply Train (Buff wildcat and border). Design painting from the records of The Institute of Heraldry.

EIGHTY-SECOND DIVISION
LINEAGE
Constituted 5 August 1917 in the National Army as Headquarters, 82ⁿᵈ Division. Organized 25 August 1917 at Camp Gordon, Georgia. Demobilized 27 May at Camp Mills, New York.
CAMPAIGN PARTICIPATION
World War I
St. Mihiel
Meuse-Argonne
Lorraine 1918
Approved: 21 October 1918 and 21 February 1919

On 20 October 1918 HQRS 82ᴺᴰ DIVISION by telegram to ADJUTANT GENERAL, A.E.F. wrote "REPLYING TO YOUR M-674 SUBMIT FOR 82ᴺᴰ DIVISION SQUARE RED CLOTH BLUE DISK SUPERIMPOSED." By telegram on 21 October 1918 G.H.Q., A.E.F. replied to Commanding General, 82d Division as follows: "Number M-694. Reference your telegram of October twentieth comma design adopted by 82d Division is approved period Submit by mail sample of design or drawing and complete description thereof comma for records of these Headquarters." On 23 October 1918 Commanding General, 82ⁿᵈ Division replied by letter to The Adjutant General, G.H.Q., American E.F. "1. In compliance with telegraphic instructions, Number M-694, G.H.Q., A.E.F., October 21ˢᵗ, herewith is submitted drawing of design to be worn by Officers and Enlisted men of the 82ⁿᵈ Division. 2. Back ground, square of red cloth, 6cms. by 6 cms.; circle of blue cloth superimposed, centers coincident. Blue circle to be 4.5 cms. in diameter, and sewed to the red back ground."

On 24 October 1918 the memorandum from General Headquarters American Expeditionary Forces setting forth "…the divisions which have submitted descriptions of the distinctive insignia adopted, and which have been approved by this office,…" described the design as: "Square red cloth, blue disk superimposed." O.Q.M.G. sheet 5-2-8 notes the approval as AG. AEF. Oct. 21, 1918 and a subsequent approval of Feb. 21, 1919. The latter was initiated by a letter of 6 February 1919 from the Adjutant General, G.H.Q., A.E.F. to Commanding General, 82ⁿᵈ Division as follows: "With reference to your telegram of October 21, 1918, in which you submitted distinctive insignia "Square of red cloth, blue disk superimposed", which was approved by telegram this office, dated same date, as the distinctive insignia for your division, and your letter of Oct. 23, 1918, copy inclosed, describing same, it is understood that a double "A" has been added to this insignia. Report is desired with the least practicable delay as to your authority for making such change." On the page in TIOH records citing that aforesaid is depicted the design and "APPROVED as the Official insignia of the 82ⁿᵈ Division signed W.P. Burnham, Major General, N.A., Commanding." (See drawing below and note the date of Aug. 1/18.) By telegram of 21 February 1919 G.H.Q., A.E.F. to Commanding General, 82ⁿᵈ Division wrote: "M-375 Change of distinctive insignia to add double "A" superimposed on blue circle as submitted by sample to these Headquarters is approved period"

On 7 July 1922, a memorandum from War Department General Staff to the Adjutant General of the Army stated "The Secretary of War directs that the drawing herewith be sent to the Quartermaster General, together with a communication in substance as follows: The shoulder sleeve insignia of the 82nd Division was approved by telegram from the Adjutant General, A. E. F. dated October 21, 1918 and February 21, 1919 to the Commanding General, 82nd Division. It is described as follows: Upon a red square 2 3/8 inches on a side a blue disc 1 3/4 inches in diameter with the letters A A in white. The inner elements of the two A's vertical lines and the outer elements arcs of a circle 1 3/8 inches in diameter, elements of letters 1/8 inch in width." It is believed the latter telegram of 21 February 1919 approved the addition of the A A (All American) to the design.

Symbolism: The double "A" refers to the nickname "All American Division."

Drawing of design inclosed with communication of 23 October 1918 of Commanding General, 82ⁿᵈ Division to The Adjutant General, G.H.Q., American E.F.

Design painting from the records of The Institute of Heraldry.

Copy of design drawing inclosed with 6 February 1919 communication of Adjutant General to Commanding General, 82nd Division. Note that it is believed the insignia was depicted in color.

Design painting from the records of the National Archives. (Letters AA should be white.)

EIGHTY-THIRD DIVISION
LINEAGE
Constituted 5 August 1917 in the National Army as Headquarters, 83d Division. Organized 25 August 1917 at Camp Sherman, Ohio. Demobilized 8 October 1919 at Camp Sherman, Ohio.
CAMPAIGN PARTICIPATION
World War I
Streamer without inscription
Approved: 26 December 1918

On 12 December 1918 a telegram was sent by Headquarters S.O.S. to C IN C HAEF "A-160 GENERAL GLENN REQUESTS THAT THE 83RD DIVISION BE AUTHORIZED TO DESIGN AND WEAR SHOULDER INSIGNIA SIMILAR TO THAT WORN BY MEMBERS OF DIVISIONS BELONGING TO 1ST ARMY PERIOD I RECOMMEND APPROVAL ON GROUND THAT IT WILL FOSTER ESPRIT DE CORPS AND HELP DISCIPLINE OF DIVISION ON ITS RETURN TO US". On 19 December Commanding General, American Embarkation Center wrote to Commanding General, S.O.S. "1 In accordance with the authority granted in telegram A-176, December 13, 1918, from Headquarters, S.O.S., I beg to submit herewith design for distinctive shoulder insignia to be worn by permanent personnel of 83rd. Division. 2. The drawing is the exact size of said insignia, and it is proposed that the scroll design shall be in gold with a back ground of either black or bottle green, depending upon the availability of latter cloth. 3. Please wire approval when granted, so that we can have these made up before the Division returns to America." By telegram on 26 December 1918 G.H.Q., A.E.F. replied to Commanding General, 83rd Division "M-1119 period Distinctive design submitted in your letter of the nineteenth instant approved for Eighty Third Division period Matter of supply of these designs should be taken up with Chief Quartermaster period".

The O.Q.M.G. sheet 5-2-8 notes approval as AG. AEF. Dec. 26, 1918. Although the 83rd Division insignia was not listed on the "LIST OF DIVISIONAL INSIGNIAS APPROVED BY GHQ TO DATE" by Office Chief Q.M. AEF of January 1, 1919, it is assumed that with the approval of 26 December 1918 the Chief Q.M. had not received the description of the design prior to the issuance of the list.

On 21 June 1922, a memorandum from War Department General Staff to the Adjutant General of the Army stated "The Secretary of War directs that the drawing herewith be sent to the Quartermaster General, together with a communication in substance as follows: The shoulder sleeve insignia of the 83rd Division was approved by telegram December 26, 1918 from the Adjutant General, A. E. F. to the Commanding General, 83rd Division. It is described as follows: On a black inverted pyramid 2 – 1/2" base and 3" slant height the cipher O H I O in yellow. The monogram consisting of two circles, the outer one 1 – 1/8" in diameter and 1/32 in width, the inner one 7/16", with one horizontal and three vertical lines. All elements within the outer circle 1/16" in width."

Symbolism: The cipher spelling OHIO refers to this division as being originally
known as the "Ohio Division."

Design drawing inclosed with 19 December 1918 communication of Commanding General, American Embarkation Center to Commanding General, S.O.S. Note: Commanding General, American Embarkation Center was Major General E.F. Glenn, also Commanding General 83rd Division.

Design painting from the records
of The Institute of Heraldry.

EIGHTY-FOURTH DIVISION
LINEAGE
    Constituted 5 August 1917 in the National Army as Headquarters, 84th Division. Organized 25 August at Camp Zachary Taylor, Kentucky. Demobilized 26 July 1919 at Camp Zachary Taylor, Kentucky.
CAMPAIGN PARTICIPATION
    World War I
        Streamer without inscription
Approved: ? 1918

    The verification of an insignia design approval by G.H.Q., A.E.F. remains an open issue, notwithstanding several specific citations of a design being approved or not authorized. Initially by General Orders No. 29 of April 14, 1918, HEADQUARTERS 84TH DIVISION states "1. The design shown below is hereby approved as the Official Divisional Insignia of the 84th Division. 2. This design will be used in all cases where any Official Divisional Insignia is required. 3. When colors are employed, the ring shall be red; the lettering and figures, blue; the head of the axe, red; the handle of the axe, blue; the background, white." A notation is written on the copy in the National Archives files "not approved".
    On 23 October 1918 a telegram from G.H.Q., A.E.F. to Commanding General, 84th Division advised "Recommendation for divisional insignia Eighty fourth Division will be submitted by General Hale direct to GHQ period". On same date Commanding General, 84th Division, Major General, Harry C. Hale, by telegram to Adjutant General, HAEF "G HQ TELEGRAM OF OCTOBER EIGHTEENTH EMBLEM RECOMMENDED FOR OLIVE IS A RAIL SPLITTERS AXE TWO AND SEVEN EIGHTS INCHES HIGH ONE AND THREE FOURTH INCHES WIDE MADE OF RED FLANNEL EDGE TO FRONT PERIOD OLIVE CALLED LINCOLN DIVISION HENCE ABOVE DEVICE". (Olive was code name for the 84th Division.) On 24 October G.H.Q., A.E.F. replied to Commanding General, 84th Division "Number M-722. Reference your telegram of October twenty-third comma submit by mail to this office sample or drawing with complete description of design selected period Upon receipt thereof decision as to approval will be made." The Red Axe design depicted below is in the records of the National Archives with the aforesaid correspondence.
    In a communication from GENERAL HEADQUARTERS AMERICAN EXPEDITIONARY FORCES INTELLIGENCE SECTION OF 17 February 1919 O.I.C., Photographic Sub-section, G-2-D to Chief, G-2-D, G.H.Q., A.E.F. wrote "1. In order to provide the historical archives with proper photographic records of the various shoulder badges used in the A.E.F., I recently obtained from Depot Quartermaster, Paris, samples of all shoulder badges he had in stock and have had them photographed and painted in colors at the Signal Corps Photographic Laboratory, Vincennes. The number of shoulder badges obtained from the Depot Quartermaster and the units they designate follow:" In the list is "84th Division". (The entire communication is included hereinbefore in ORIGIN AND EVOLUTION OF SHOULDER SLEEVE INSIGNIA – WORLD WAR I.)
    In the TIOH files is a copy of a 24 April 1919 letter from Office of the Surgeon, Bassens District, Capt. C.P. Chinn, San. C. to Adjutant General, A.E.F. as follows: "1. Request information regarding the wearing of Divisional Insignia of the 84th Division. Although I

have never seen an official publication of the 84th Divisional Insignia it is understood that it is as follows:- A circle of red with a white field, superimposed small axe, the blade red, the handle blue, at top superimposed in blue letters of word "Lincoln" and at the bottom the number "84". This insignia is being worn by a large number of men who formerly belonged to the 84th Division. 2. The 84th Division has been returned to the United States for demobilization. 3. Am I as an officer serving in the A. E. F. and attached to no division entitled to wear the official insignia of the 84th Division?" By 1st. Ind. on April 28, 1919 G.H.Q., American E. F. replied "Distinctive cloth insignia for the 84th Division was never authorized by these headquarters." Also noted in the files of the National Archives is a hand written notation "In reply to a letter by the CO 309th Engineers the AG replied on 5/12/1919 that "A distinctive insignia was never authorized by these Headquarters for the 84th Division".

However, on the "LIST OF DIVISIONAL INSIGNIAS APPROVED BY GHQ TO DATE" by Office Chief Q.M. AEF of January 1, 1919, the 84th Div. is listed with an insignia of a "Red Hatchet." Also, in the 19 November 1919 Memorandum of General Headquarters American Expeditionary Forces hereinbefore noted in paragraph "3. The following mistakes are noted. (a) The insignia of the 84th Division as approved, is attached." It is believed the drawing attached to the reply of Commanding General, 84th Division to the 24 October 1918 telegram M-722 of G.H.Q., A.E.F. was inclosed. Furthermore, on a copy of General Orders, Headquarters 84th Division of April 14, 1918, depicting a design consistent with the description in the 24 April 1919 letter of Dr. Chinn there is a written notation "not approved."

Design painting in the records
of the National Archives.

Design drawing included with the "DOCUMENT FILE" of the National Archives and conforming to the description in 23 October 1918 telegram of Commanding General, 84th Division to Adjutant General, HAEF.

EIGHTY-FIFTH DIVISION
LINEAGE
    Constituted 5 August 1917 in the National Army as Headquarters, 85th Division. Organized 25 August 1917 at Camp Custer, Michigan. Demobilized 18 April 1919 at Camp Custer, Michigan.
CAMPAIGN PARTICIPATION
    World War I
        Streamer without inscription
Approved: 24 December 1918

    On 6 November1918 Commanding General, 85th Division by telegram to ADJUTANT GENERAL G HQ AEF wrote "FOLLOWING SLEEVE DESIGN RECOMMANDED FOR EIGHTY FIFTH DIVISION COLON LETTERS C D FORMED BY CONCENTRIC CIRCLES WITH VERTICLE BREAK THROUGH CENTER PERIOD NAME CUSTER DIVISION ADOPTED IN UNITED STATES AND ABOVE DESIGN USED IN MARKING ALL FREIGHT AND BAGGAGE OF DIVISION". On 6 November, by a 1st Ind. G.H.Q., A.E.F. advised Commanding General, 85th Division "It is not contemplated to authorize insignia for Depot Divisions." By a 2nd Ind. of 22 December 1918 Hq. 85th Div. to The Adjutant General, G. H. Q., A. E. F. wrote "1. It is requested that this decision be reconsidered. 2. The 85th Division was in existence as a division for about a year before it was broken up. It had a fine espirit de Corps; its officers and men were proud to belong to it. The name Custer Division was adopted both to show the locality from which the men came and as an incentive to emulate the qualities of courage and self-sacrifice exemplified by the life of that distinguished soldier. A design, of which a copy is inclosed, was adopted to show briefly the name selected for the division. 3. Since its arrival in France the 85th Division has furnished 542 officers and 14960 men to combat divisions. They have done their share in helping to make the operations of the American Army in the field a success. The remaining officers and men of the division, though deprived of the privilege of doing the work for which they have been trained, have done the work assigned them faithfully and uncomplainingly. They still take pride in belonging to the Custer Division, and wish to wear an insignia to show it. I believe they are entitled to more consideration than is shown in the curt refusal in the 1st Indorsement." By telegram of 24 December 1918 G.H.Q., A.E.F. replied to Commanding General, 85th Division "M-1101. Distinctive design submitted by your 2nd indorsement December 22nd approved. Matter of supply of insignia should be taken up with C. Q. M." On 25 December 1918 HEADQUARTERS FOURTH DEPOT DIVISION issued Memorandum No. 79 "1. The following distinctive design has been approved by G. H. Q. for the 85th Division: DESIGN Color - - Red. Officers will take immediate steps to provide themselves with the insignia. The Division Quartermaster will take up with the Chief Quartermaster, A. E. F., Tours, the matter of supplying insignia to enlisted men." On 26 December Memorandum No. 80 was issued as follows: "1. Memorandum No. 79, these headquarters, dated Dec. 25th, 1918, is amended to read that the Distinctive Design will be of SCARLET color and mounted on a circle of O.D. cloth, 1/4" larger than the Design."
    On 21 June 1922, a memorandum from War Department General Staff to the Adjutant General of the Army stated "The Secretary of War directs that the drawing herewith be sent to the Quartermaster General, together with a communication in substance as follows:

The shoulder sleeve insignia of the 85th Division was approved by telegram December 24, 1918 from the Adjutant General, A. E. F. to the Commanding General, 85th Division. It is described as follows: Upon an olive drab disc 2 1/4" in diameter the letters "C D" in scarlet. The curves of the two letters being the arcs of a circle 1 – 7/8" in diameter. The elements of the letters 3/16" in width."

Symbolism: The letters "C D" symbolized "Custer Division," a nickname derived from the formation of the division at Camp Custer, Michigan, and are an incentive to emulate the qualities of courage and self sacrifice exemplified by the life of Major General George H. Custer.

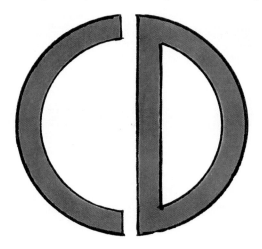

Design painting from the records
of the National Archives.

Sample from the records of the National Archives conforming to the description in Memorandum No. 80 of Headquarters Fourth Depot Division, 26 December 1918.

Design drawing accompanying 22 December 1918 2ⁿᵈ Ind. of Hq. 85ᵗʰ Div. to the Adjutant General, G.H.Q., A.E.F. and approved by telegram M-1101.

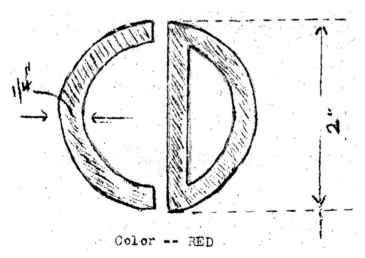

Color -- RED

Design drawing depicted on 25 December 1918 Headquarters Fourth Depot Division Memorandum No. 79.

EIGHTY-SIXTH DIVISION
LINEAGE
   Constitute 5 August 1917 in the National Army as Headquarters and Headquarters Troop, 86th Division. Organized 25 August 1917 at Camp Grant, Illinois. Demobilized in January 1919 at Camp Grant, Illinois.
CAMPAIGN PARTICIPATION
   World War I
      Streamer without inscription
Approved: 26 November 1918

   On 13 November 1918 G.H.Q., A.E.F. advised Commanding General, 86th Division and Commanding General, 91st Division by telegram Number M-851 that each Division was to adopt and submit to G.H.Q., A.E.F. for approval a distinctive cloth design to be worn on the left arm. period ..." On 14 November 1918 Hq. 86th Division replied to ADJT GENERAL HAEF by telegram "NUMBER THREE D PERIOD A PERIOD RE TEL NUMBER M EIGHT FIFTY ONE PERIOD RECOMMEND AS DESIGN FOR EIGHTY SIXTH DIVISION PERIOD RED INDIAN HEAD ON BLACK SHIELD PERIOD". On same date G.H.Q., A.E.F. by telegram replied to Commanding General, 86th Division "Number M-858. Reference your telegram number three D comma Indian head design submitted as insignia for 86th Division cannot be approved having already been selected by 2d Division period Another design will be selected and reported by wire to this office for consideration comma sample or drawing with complete description thereof to be sent by mail for records of these Headquarters." On 17 November 1918 Commanding Officer, 86th Division wrote Adjutant General, Haef by telegram "Number twenty two D period A period re tel number M eight fifty eight recommend as insignia for eighty sixth division quote red shield with black eagle with superimposed red shield and initials B period H period upon approval of insignia will mail drawing." By return telegram from G.H.Q., A.E.F. to Commanding General, 86th Division wrote "M-880. Reference you telegram two two D. A. Mail drawing of design selected for Division and decision as to approval will then made by these headquarters." On 21 November Commanding Officer, 86th Division wrote The Adjutant General, HAEF "1. Reference you telegram M 858 dated November 14th, and M 880 dated November 17th, submit for approval as insignia for the 86th Division Red Shield with Black Eagle, with Superimposed Red Shield and Initials "B.H.", as per attached drawing." On 26 November 1918 G.H.Q, A.E.F. replied to Commanding General, 86th Division "M-931 Reference your letter of November twenty first comma design submitted as distinctive insignia for Eighty sixth Division is approved period".
   On 11 July 1922, a memorandum from War Department General Staff to the Adjutant General of the Army stated "The Secretary of War directs that the drawing herewith be sent to the Quartermaster General, together with a communication in substance as follows: The shoulder sleeve insignia of the 86th Division was approved by telegram November 26, 1918 from the Adjutant General, A. E. F. to the Commanding General, 86th Division. It is described as follows: Upon a red triangular shield 2 ½ inches high and 2 ¼ inches wide, a black hawk displayed. On a red shield on the hawks breast the letters "B H" bendwise in black."

Symbolism: The black hawk with the initials "B H" superimposed on the red
shield is symbolic of the nickname of the division, "Black Hawk Division."

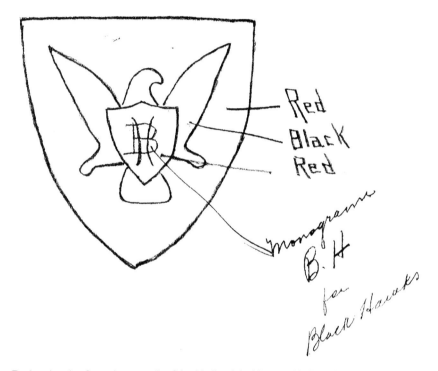

Design drawing from the records of the National Archives and believed to be that inclosed with 21 November 1918 communication of Commanding General, 86th Division to The Adjutant General, HAEF. Note that the Eagle is facing to the Eagle's left, however, the known samples of the WWI era insignia observed by the author have depicted the Eagle facing to the right, forward when sewn on the left sleeve.

Drawing from the records of the National Archives.

Design painting from the records of the National Archives.

EIGHTY-SEVENTH DIVISION
LINEAGE
    Constituted 5 August 1917 in the National Army as Headquarters and Headquarters Troop, 87th Division. Organized 25 August 1917 at Camp Pike, Arkansas. Demobilized 14 February 1919 at Camp Dix, New Jersey.
CAMPAIGN PARTICIPATION
    World War I
        Streamer without inscription
Approved: 9 November 1918

    On 19 October 1918 G.H.Q., A.E.F. advised Commanding General, 84th Division and Commanding General, 87th Division by telegram Number M-680 that each Division was to adopt and submit to G.H.Q., A.E.F. for approval a distinctive cloth design to be worn on the left arm.. On 2 November 1918 by telegram G.H.Q., A.E.F. to C G, 87th Divn wrote "Number M 783 reference your telegram three six five comma submit by mail without delay sample or drawing with complete description of design adopted period Upon receipt thereof decision as to approval will be telegraphed you period". In reply on same date Commanding General, 87th Division wrote Commanding General, G. H. Q., American E. F. "1. Pursuant to instructions in your telegram M 783, a drawing of the insignia adopted by this Division is enclosed. 2. The drawing is actual size, the green background being 2 ½ inches in diameter and the acorn 1 ½ inches long." On 9 November 1918 G.H.Q., A.E.F. wrote to commanding General, 87th Division "Number M-824. Reference your letter of November second comma design adopted as insignia for Eighty-seventh Division is approved."
    In reply to a request for confirmation of the 87th Division design from Acting Chief of Staff to Quartermaster General of 18 February 1922, the Adjutant General of the Army replied to the Quartermaster General: "The shoulder sleeve insignia of the 87th Division is described as follows: On a green disc 2 1/4" in diameter a yellow acorn stem up."

Symbolism: The acorn is a symbol of the strength of the division.

Design drawing inclosed with 2 November 1918 communication of Commanding General, 87th Division to Commanding General, G.H.Q., A.E.F. Description:"Green background Brown Acorn 1 ½ inch 2 ½ " diameter."

EIGHTY-EIGHTH DIVISION
LINEAGE
Constituted 5 August 1917 in the National Army as Headquarters and Headquarters Troop, 88th Division. Organized 25 August 1917 at Camp Dodge, Iowa. Demobilized 10 June 1919 at Camp Dodge, Iowa.
CAMPAIGN PARTICIPATION
World War I
Alsace 1918
Approved: 21 October 1918 and 12 November 1918

On 21 October 1918 Commanding General, 87th Division wrote ADJUTANT GENERAL HEADQUARTERS AMERICAN E F "A EIGHT NAUGHT PERIOD RE YOUR TELG NN YOUR TELEGRAM NUMBER M SIX SEVEN FOUR FOLLOWING DESIGN SUBMITTED FOR SUSAN DIVISION PERIOD TWO ELONGATED FIGURES EIGHT CROSSING AT RIGHT ANGLES TO EACH OTHER GIVING THE APPEARANCE OF A MALTESE CROSS MADE OF LOOPS PERIOD WILL DIMENSIONS AND COLOR BE PRESCRIBED BY YOUR HEADQUARTERS QUESTION." (Susan was code name for the 88th Division.) In reply, on 21 October G.H.Q., A.E.F. to Commanding General, 88th Division wrote "Number M-700. Reference your telegram A 80 comma design adopted by 88th Division is approved period Dimensions and color will be prescribed by Division Commander period Submit by mail sample of design or drawing and complete description thereof for records of these Headquarters." On 12 November 1918 G.H.Q., A.E.F advised Commanding General, 88th Division by telegram "Number M-847. Reference your telegram A 80 comma design adopted by 88th Division is approved period Dimensions and color will be prescribed by Division Commander period Submit by mail sample of design or drawing and complete description thereof for records of these Headquarters." The same date Commanding General, 88th Division wrote Adjutant General, G.H.Q., A.E.F. "1. Reference telegram No. M-847, sample of design of distinctive insignia 88th Division to be worn on left shoulder is enclosed herewith. 2. The design consists of two figures "8" crossing at right angles to each other giving the appearance of a Maltese cross made of loops. Extreme height of design is 2 1/4 inches; extreme width of loops 7/8 inch. The colors prescribed are:

> For infantry brigades and division machine gun battalion, navy blue
> For artillery brigade, red
> For divisional troops and special units, black."

Attached to the letter was a blue sample paper cut out of the design.
Attached on the 12 September 1918 approving telegram copy on file was a black melton wool sample.
Also, on 12 November 1918 HEADQUARTERS 88TH DIVISION issued GENERAL ORDERS No. 80 as follows: "I. 1. The design of distinctive insignia to be worn on left shoulder with the top of the insignia at the shoulder seam of sleeve of coat, has been approved for the 88th Division and is published for the information of all concerned. It is two figures "8" crossing at right angles to each other giving the appearance of a Maltese cross made of loops. The extreme height of the design is 2 1/4 inches; the extreme width of loops is 7/8 inch. The colors prescribed are:

For infantry brigades and divisional machine gun battalion, navy blue.

For Artillery brigade, red.

For divisional troops and special units, black.

2. Pending the receipt of necessary insignia upon requisition, the Commanding Generals of brigades and the Commanding Officers of special units will take the necessary steps at once to provide their troops with their particular insignia. As cloth of the prescribed color may not be readily available, a temporary expedient will be adopted by using khaki or olive drab or some other colored cloth cut according to pattern. 3. All officers and men of the Division will have the authorized insignia of the proper shape and as near the prescribed color as possible on their uniforms by November 20th, 1918."

On 24 October 1918 the memorandum from General Headquarters American Expeditionary Forces setting forth "...the divisions which have submitted descriptions of the distinctive insignia adopted, and which have been approved by this office,..." described the design as: "Two figures "8" crossing at right angles to each other giving the appearance of a Maltese cross made of loops."

On 27 June 1922, a memorandum from War Department General Staff to the Adjutant General of the Army stated "The Secretary of War directs that the drawing herewith be sent to the Quartermaster General, together with a communication in substance as follows: The shoulder sleeve insignia of the 88th Division was approved by telegram November 12, 1918 from the Adjutant General, A. E. F. to the Commanding General, 88th Division. It is described as follows: A blue quatrefoil (two figure 8's crossing at right angles) 2 1/4 inches in height, width of loops 7/8 inch."

Symbolism: The four leaf clover, formed by the two figures "8", represents the Dakotas, Minnesota, Iowa, and Illinois, from which personnel of the division originally came.

Design drawing inclosed with 12 November 1918 communication of Commanding General, 88th Division to Adjutant General, G.H.Q., A.E.F. The drawing is the navy blue designation of the infantry brigades and division machine gun battalion.

Drawing red representing the artillery brigade.

Drawing black representing divisional troops and special units.

EIGHTY-NINTH DIVISION
LINEAGE

Constituted 5 August 1917 in the National Army ass Headquarters, 89ᵗʰ Division. Organized 13 August 1917 at Camp Funston, Kansas. Demobilized 12 June 1919 at Camp Funston, Kansas.

CAMPAIGN PARTICIPATION

World War I

St. Mihiel

Meuse-Argonne

Lorraine 1918

Approved: 25 October 1918

On 19 October 1918 Division Commander, 89ᵗʰ Division wrote Commanding General, 1ˢᵗ Army "1. In compliance with telegram No. 194, Secretary G. S. (Through 5ᵗʰ Corps), I submit herewith design of divisional insignia to be worn on the left shoulder. 2. This should be cut out of black broadcloth or felt and sewed on olive drab cloth. 3. This insignia has been in use by the division for several months and its transportation, etc., has been marked with it. It is the insignia recognized in and by the division." Following paragraph 1.of the letter is a drawing of the insignia as shown below. On 25 October 1918 by telegram to ADJUTANT GENERAL, GHQ AEF from HEADQUARTERS 89ᵗʰ DIVN wrote "NO M SIX SEVEN FOUR DASH DIVISION SHOULDER DESIGN IS A BLACK W WITHIN A CIRCLE PERIOD DESIGN FOLLOWS WITH MAIL COPY DASH TWENTY FOUR". By telegram of same date G.H.Q., A.E.F. to Commanding General, 89ᵗʰ Division wrote "Number M-732. Reference your letter of October nineteenth to Commanding General 1ˢᵗ Army comma design adopted by 89ᵗʰ Division as Divisional insignia is approved."

Subsequently, on 15 February 1919 G.H.Q., A.E.F. wrote C.G.89ᵗʰ Divn. "The C. in-Chief directs that you furnish with the least practicably delay, to the commanding Gen. SOS a sample of the distinctive insignia authorized for your command with complete description and dimensions." In reply by 1ˢᵗ. Ind. of 26 February 1919 Hq. 89ᵗʰ Divn. AEF A O 761. to the Adjt.Gen.GHQ.AEF. wrote "1. A sample of the shoulder piece used in this division is attached, together with copies of the Divn. orders showing the development of the D ivn. ins. from the original conception in Aug. 1918, to the perfected form described in later G.O."

Although a memorandum of 6 August 1918 of HEADQUARTERS MIDDLE WEST DIVISION prescribed that certain letters and symbols were to identify units of the division on "property including rolling stock and large equipment", and by General Orders No. 77 of 30 September 1918 provided that "1. Hereafter the Division insignia will be worn on both sides of the trench helmet by members of the Division", and that units of the division would display various colors on the center of the design. No evidence was found that such sub-unit designations were approved for inclusion on the distinctive shoulder cloth insignia of the 89ᵗʰ Division, although it is well known that such variations were worn.

On 21 June 1922, a memorandum from War Department General Staff to the Adjutant General of the Army stated "The Secretary of War directs that the drawing herewith be sent to the Quartermaster General, together with a communication in substance as follows: The shoulder sleeve insignia of the 89th Division was approved by telegram October 25,

1918 from the Adjutant General, A. E. F. to the Commanding General, 89th Division. It is described as follows: On an olive drab disc 2 1/4" in diameter a black circle 2" in diameter and 3/16" in width the letter "W" formed of curved lines 3/16" in width and touching the circle."

Symbolism: The stylized "W" when reserved becomes an "M," and refers to the division being known as the "Middle West Division," since many of its personnel came from the Midwestern states.

Drawing depicted on 19 October 1918 communication of Division Commander, 89th Division to Commanding General, 1st Army and approved by G.H.Q., A.E.F. telegram M-732.

Sample from the records of the National Archives.

NINETIETH DIVISION
LINEAGE

Constituted 5 August 1917 in the National Army as Headquarters, 90th Division. Organized 25 August 1917 at Camp Travis, Texas. Demobilized 17 June 1919 at Camp Bowie, Texas

CAMPAIGN PARTICIPATION

World War I

St. Mihiel

Meuse-Argonne

Lorraine 1918

Approved: 25 October 1918

On 20 October 1918 Commanding General, 90th Division advised ADJUTANT GENERAL HAEF by telegram "RETEL M SIX SEVEN FOUR DESIGN SELECTED TO THIS DIVISION IS MONOGRAM TO BLOCK LETTER RECEIVED CLOTH". On 21 October G.H.Q., A.E.F. replied to Commanding General, 90th Division by telegram "Number M-693. Reference your telegram of October twentieth relative insignia for 90th Division comma submit drawing or sample of design to this office without delay period Upon receipt of this comma decision as to approval will be wired you." On same date Commanding General, 90th Division wrote Adjutant General, H. A. E.. F. "1. Reference your telegram No. 5-693, herewith is design of insignia proposed to adopt for this division. The letters of T. O. represent states of Texas and Oklahoma, from which this division was drawn." The design was attached. On 25 October 1918 by telegram of G.H.Q., A.E.F. to Commanding General, 90th Division advised "Number M-733. Reference your letter of October twenty-first comma design submitted is approved as insignia for 90th Division." Attached to a copy of the telegram in the National Archives is a red cut out of the TO in wool without a background. Also, on file in the National Archives is an undated communication titled "DESCRIPTION AND DIMENSIONS DISTINCTIVE INSIGNIA 90TH DIVISION" as follows: "The insignia of the 90th Division is a combination of the letters "T" and "O", the "T" being symbolic of TEXAS and the "O" of OKLAHOMA. This division is composed of men from there two states.

Dimensions are as follows:

From top to bottom of the letters "TO"   1 ¾ inches.

Width   1 ¾ inches

This insignia is placed upon a background of O. D. cloth in the shape of a shield with the corners slightly rounded at the top and rounded to a point at the bottom.

Dimensions as follows:

From middle of top to bottom of shield   2 7/16 inches.

Width   2 1/8 inches."

Symbolism: The "O T" monogram refers to Oklahoma and Texas, home states of many of the original personnel of the division.

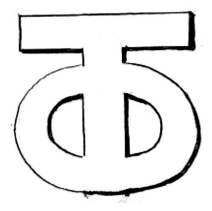

Design drawing depicted on 21 October 1918 communication of Commanding General, 90th Division to Adjutant General, H.A.E.F.

Sample attached to the copy of approval telegram M-733 of 25 October 1918. From the records of the National Archives.

Sample from the records of the National Archives.

NINETY-FIRST DIVISION
    Constituted 5 August in the National Army as Headquarters, 91ˢᵗ Division. Organized 26 August at Camp Lewis, Washington. Demobilized 13 May 1919 at the Presidio of San Francisco, California.
CAMPAIGN PARTICIPATION
    World War I
        Ypres-Lys
        Meuse-Argonne
        Lorraine 1918
Approved:8 December 1918

    On 13 November 1918 G.H.Q., A.E.F. advised Commanding General, 86th Division and Commanding General, 91ˢᵗ Division by telegram "Number M-851. Each Division will adopt and procure immediately some distinctive cloth design which will be worn by every officer and man of the division on the upper left arm period The upper part to be attached to the shoulder seam period Report will be made to these Headquarters by telegram as to design adopted and in order that there may be no duplications approval will be made by telegram from there Headquarters."
    On 16 November 1918 the Commanding General, 91ˢᵗ Division wrote The Adjutant General, American E. F. "1. In compliance with telegram number 857, there is submitted herewith a design of a distinguishing insignia to be worn by the 91ˢᵗ Division on the left shoulder of the service coat. This design is a fir tree to be made of green cloth, as per the sample herewith, being typical of the States to which the majority from this Division belong. 2. The tree is inscribed in a triangle, the base of which is two inches and the altitude two inches with a trunk one-half inch long and one-fourth inch wide. 3. Information is requested as to whether, upon approval of this design, material will be furnished by the Quartermaster Corps or whether it is to be procured by the organizations." Attached to the letter in the National Archives is a green wool fir tree, although the dimensions are 2 1/2" and 2" in width with a trunk 1/2" long and 1/4" wide, and also on file a drawing of similar dimensions dated "Belgium Nov 14, 1918". By telegram of G.H.Q., A.E.F. on 8 December 1918 to C. G., 91ˢᵗ Div. advised "Number M 990 period Reference your letter November xxx sixteenth colon Distinctive design submitted is approved for your division period Matter of supply of these designs should be taken up with Chief Quartermaster."
    On 13 December 1918 HQ. 91ˢᵀ Div. issued GENERAL ORDERS: No. 57. "1. The following distinctive insignia has been adopted for all officers and men of this Division, to be worn on the left shoulder with the top of the insignia one inch below the shoulder seam of the service coat: A fir tree of green cloth to conform to sample on file in the office of the Division quartermaster. The tree is inscribed in a triangle, the base of which is two (2) inches and the altitude two (2) inches, with a trunk one-half (1/2) inch long and one-quarter inch wide, to conform to sketch below" DESIGN The Division Quartermaster will take the necessary steps to provide this insignia with the least practicable delay." The "DESIGN" was not observed in the records reviewed.

On 20 June 1922, a memorandum from War Department General Staff to the Adjutant General of the Army stated "The Secretary of War directs that the drawing herewith be sent to the Quartermaster General, together with a communication in substance as follows: The shoulder sleeve insignia of the 91st Division was approved by telegram December 8, 1918 from the Adjutant General, A. E. F. to the Commanding General, 91st Division. It is described as follows: A green conventionalized fir tree approximately 2 – 1/2" in height and 2" in width."

Sample attached to 16 November 1918 communication of the Commanding General, 91st Division to The Adjutant General, American E.F.

Drawing "Symbolic of Design 91st Div. Belgium Nov.14, 1918" inclosed with the 16 November 1918 communication of the Commanding General, 91st Division to The Adjutant General, American E.F.

NINETY-SECOND DIVISION
LINEAGE
    Constituted 24 October 1917 in the National Army as Headquarters and Headquarters
Troop, 92d Division. Organized 29 October 1917 at Camp Funston, Kansas. Demobilized
7 March 1919 at Camp Upton, New York.
CAMPAIGN PARTICIPATION
    World War I
        Meuse-Argonne
        Lorraine 1918
Approved: 20 October 1918 and 16 December 1918

    On 19 October 1918 by telegram from HQRS 92nd Divn to Adjutant General, General
Headquarters A E F wrote "Number nine seven four period distinctive cloth design buffalo
adopted for division". By telegram of 20 October 1918 G.H.Q., A.E.F. to Commanding
General, 92nd Division replied "M-684. Reference your telegram nine seven four October
nineteenth the design of Buffalo adopted by Ninety-second Division is approved." On
16 November 1918 G.H.Q., A.E.F. advised Commanding General, 92nd Division by
telegram "Number M-862. Reference your telegram nine seven four of October nineteenth
submit by mail to this office without delay sample or drawing with complete description
of Buffalo design adopted by Ninety-second Division." On 12 December 1918 G.H.Q.,
A.E.F. telegrammed Commanding General, 92nd Division "M-1018 Send sample of cloth
design adopted by your division to these headquarters with least practicable delay period."
On 15 December 1918 Commanding General, 92nd Division wrote to Adjutant General,
GHQ, Am.E.F. "1. Enclosed are the color samples of division insignia made up for 92nd
Division. 2. The red background is for artillery, blue for infantry and buff for the staff.
The buff should be much lighter shade and better cut. 3. Sketches of the design have been
forwarded heretofore and the enclosed are roughly made samples of cloth in compliance
with your telegram M 1018 of December 12, 1918. 4. This division has been ordered to
Port of Embarkation and will leave shortly for the United States. If insignia is to be worn by
troops of this division they must be made and sent to the division before sailing which will
be approximately on January 1, 1919." By telegram of 16 December 1918 from G.H.Q.,
A.E.F. to Commanding General 92nd Division advised "M-1039 Reference your telegram
seventeen G dash one period Cloth design selected by your division is approved but the
matter of supply of these designs should be taken up with the Chief Quartermaster at Tours
period"
    On 7 July 1922, a memorandum from War Department, The Adjutant General of the
Army to The Quartermaster General stated "1. The shoulder sleeve insignia for the 92nd
Division was approved by telegrams dated October 20, 1918 and December 6, 1918, from
the Adjutant General, A. E. F. to the Commanding General, 92nd Division. It is described
as follows: Within a black circle 2 1/4 inches in diameter and 1/8 of an inch in width upon
an olive drab disc a black buffalo statant." (The noted date of December 6, 1918, is an
apparent error for the telegram dated December 16, 1918, aforesaid.)

Symbolism: The buffalo refers to the nickname of the division.

Design painting from the records of the National Archives.

Drawing buff for the staff.

Drawing red for artillery.

Drawing blue for infantry.

NINETY-THIRD DIVISION (PROVISIONAL)
LINEAGE

Constituted 23 November 1917 (? Date). Organized in December 1917 at Camp Stuart, Virginia with troops from colored National Guard units from New Your, Illinois, Connecticut, Maryland, Massachusetts, Ohio, Tennessee, and the District of Columbia and colored selective service men from South Carolina. The division was never formally demobilized but listed as discontinued in May 1918

The four infantry regiments (the 369th, 370th, 371st and 372d) were assigned to French divisions, and remained with the French Army throughout the war. Thus, the division per se has no campaign participation record.

Approved: 30 December 1918

On 27 December Commanding Officer, 371st Infantry wrote Adjutant General American E.F. "1. The enclosed pattern for arm insignia for the regiments which have been serving in French divisions is recommended by Colonel Tupes, commanding the 372nd Infantry and myself. Efforts have been made to communicate with Commanding Officer 370th Infantry by telegram but without success. Enclosed is a copy of a telegram from Commanding Officer 369th Infantry indicating concurrence in the recommendation for the insignia herewith proposed for the 93rd Provisional Division unless separate regimental insignia were permitted them, which I understand will not be done. 2. Description of insignia:- A French helmet in uniform blue two inches in length by one inch in height on a circular disk of plain black cloth 2 ½ inches in diameter. The insignia is symbolic of the service of these regiments with French divisions and urgently recommended." On 30 December 1918 the Adjutant General, G.H.Q., A.E.F. wrote to Commanding Officer, 369th Infantry, 370th Infantry, 371st Infantry, 372nd Infantry: "The following distinctive insignia proposed for the regiments of the former 93rd Division (the 369th, 370th, 371st and 372nd Infantry), is approved: Description of insignia: A French helmet in uniform blue two inches in length by one inch in height on a circular disk of plain black cloth 2 ½ inches in diameter. The insignia is symbolic of the service of these regiments with French Divisions."

Symbolism: The French helmet refers to the service of the regiments with the French Army.

Drawing from the records of the National Archives
with notation "Enlarge circle and helmet."

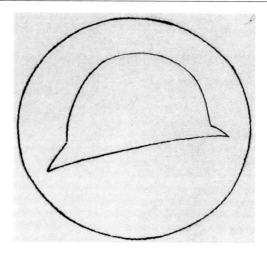

Design drawing from the records of the National Archives. Note that the helmet is tilted to be lower on the left, however, the known samples of the WWI era insignia observed by the author have depicted the helmet lower on the right, facing forward when sewn on the left sleeve.

Design painting from the records of the National Archives.

Service and Other Units

SERVICES OF SUPPLY – BASE SECTIONS
Created 5 July 1917 by G.H.Q., A.E.F. General Order No. 8 as Line of Communications to be under a Commanding General with territorial command over supply, sanitation, and telegraphic services, as well as construction and a newly formed Transportation Department. The L. of C. was organized in Base Sections, Intermediate Section, and Advance Section. On 25 July 1917 Brigadier General R. M. Bletchford was named the initial Commanding General, L. of C. On 16 February 1918 G.H.Q., A.E.F. by General Order No. 31 reorganized the G.H.Q. staff organization and renamed the Line of Communications as Service of the Rear. However, on 13 March 1918 it was redesignated as Services of Supply. As reorganized the S. O. S. consisted of:

Quartermaster Corps;
Medical Department;
Corps of Engineers;
Ordnance Department;
Signal Corps;
Air Service;
General Purchasing Board;
Gas Service;
Service of Utilities;
Provost Marshall Service;

The main change in this organization over that under the Line of Communication was the creation of the Service of Utilities, under which were grouped: (a) The Transportation Department; (b) The Department of Construction and Forestry; (c) The Department of Light Railways and Roads; and (d) The Department of Motor Transportation.

Subsequently, the Gas Service was reorganized and the Chemical Warfare Service created by G.H.Q., A.E.F. General Order No. 105 of 28 June 1918; the Military Police Corps was created by G.H.Q., A.E.F. General Order No. 111 of 8 July 1918; and the Motor Transport Corps was created as a separate and distinct corps by G.H.Q., A.E.F. General Order No. 114 of 11 July 1918, which also abolished the Service of Utilities.
SSI Approved: 24 December 1918 and 25 January 1919

On 13 December 1918 the Base Commander, Services of Supply Headquarters Base Section No 1 wrote the Commanding General, S.O.S. "There is a feeling among the officers and men who have been on duty in Base Section No 1 that they would like to have a distinctive insignia similar to those worn by officers and men attached to various divisions. 2. It would seem that this would be in the interest of good spirit among these officers and men, and I suggest that it be approved, if possible." By a 1ˢᵗ Ind. Hq. S.O.S. to C-in-C American E.F. wrote "1. Forwarded, approved, providing similar authority be granted to other section commanders in the S.O.S. 2. There has been distinct let down in enthusiasm and interest since the signing of the armistice which, however natural, is detrimental to efficient work. Any measures that can be taken to revive that interest and stimulate enthusiasm are well-worth while and should be adopted. 3. If these views meet with the approval of G.H.Q., I will have proper shoulder insignia forwarded for approval." By 2ⁿᵈ Ind. dated 24 December 1918 G.H.Q., American E.F. replied "Approved. Designs will be submitted this office for approval with least practical delay." On 25 January 1919 Hq. S.O.S. replied by 3rd Ind. "1. Returned, with a design enclosed herewith which is intended for all Sections of the S.O.S., except the Advanced Section. An identification shoulder mark has already been adopted for the Advance Section." A sample design was attached. On 25 January 1919, by telegram to C. G., S.O.S. G.H.Q., A.E.F. advised "M-196 period. Distinctive design recommended by you for Base Sections is approved."

On 6 February 1919, Headquarters Services Of Supply issued General Orders, No. 7 as follows: "I. The following information and instructions with reference to the official shoulder insignia adopted for all units of the S.O.S., with the exception of the Advance Section and the District of Paris, are published for the guidance of all concerned: 1. The insignia consists of the letters SOS in red, superimposed on blue cloth, and worn directly beneath the shoulder seam of the left arm. The wearing of this insignia is optional for use by all officers, soldiers, field clerks, army nurses and civilian employees of this command. 2. The significance of the "SOS" is known throughout the world as a call sent out for assistance from those in distress, and whenever called upon by our combatant troops we never failed to respond promptly and cheerfully. The S.O.S. was, in fact, the keystone of the arch of the American E.F., without which the structure could not have withstood the enormous pressure placed upon it. 3. The red color of the letters represents the sincerity of our endeavors, as well as the tireless devotion of the soldier back of the fighting line towards his comrade at the front. The blue back-ground represents the solid basis of the trust worthiness and faithfulness of our entire personnel. 4. There being no independent unit in the S.O.S., team work being the prime factor of our success, other insignia will not be worn. 5. Properly approved requisitions will be submitted through prescribed channels to the Chief Quartermaster, S.O.S., for supply. ..."

Symbolism: See above.

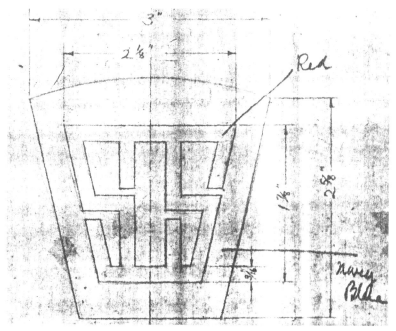

Design drawing inclosed with 23 (?25) January 1919 3rd Ind. of Hq. S.O.S. to C in C G.H.Q.

Design drawing from the records of the National Archives.

SERVICES OF SUPPLY – ADVANCE SECTION
SSI Approved: 3 February 1919

On 1 January 1919 Headquarters Advance Section, Services of Supply issued General Orders No. 1 as follows: "In view of the long services of the Advanced section, S.O.S. in Lorraine and the fact that our Headquarters have been, and now is located in the Chateau of the Duke of Lorraine, the following is adopted as a distinctive mark which may be worn on the left shoulder by all Advance Section troops: "An Army Blue circle, approximately two and one-half inches in diameter and one-eighth of an inch in width, enclosing a Steel Gray field upon which will be embroidered in red, or let into a background of red, as the case may be, a Lorraine Cross, two inches in heighth with lower half of the upright thereof flanked by the letters "A" and "S", the letters conforming to the circle of the border. The same design will be worn on the cap in the usual place: (the design shown) Details and dimensions will be in accordance with the drawing herewith." On 6 January 1919 a "Corrected Copy" of the orders were issued correcting the description as follows: "An Army Blue Circle, approximately two and one-half inches in diameter and one-eighth of an inch in width, enclosing a Pearl Gray field upon which will be embroidered in red, or let into a background of red, a Lorraine Cross two inches in heighth with lower half of the upright thereof flanked by the letters "A" and "S", the letters conforming to the circle of the border." A dotted sketch was included as depicted below. On 9 January 1919 the Adjutant General, S.O.S. wrote to Commanding General, Advance Section "1. Receipt is acknowledged of G.O. No.1, c.s., your headquarters, prescribing a distinctive shoulder mark for troops belonging to the Advance Section. 2. No authority is quoted for the adoption of such insignia, but it is presumed that you did not act without the authority of G.H.Q. In any event formal confirmation of the insignia will be published in orders shortly to be issued from these headquarters. When this is done you can submit requisition to these headquarters, and the necessary number of insignia will be supplied by the Quartermaster Corps."

Design drawing depicted on 6 January 1919 Headquarters, Advance Section, Services of Supply, General Orders No.1.

Sample from the collection
of The Johnson Brothers.

However, on 17 January 1919 Commanding General 79th Division, wrote Adjt. Gen. GHQ, AEF "1. In view of the fact that the Lorraine Cross has been authorized as the official insignia of the 79th Division (by telegraphic authority No. M. 865 Nov. 13th, 1918, signed Davis) attention is invited to the enclosed copy of G.O. No. 1, Hqrs. Advance Sect. SOS, in which it is noted that the Lorraine Cross has been adopted as their distinctive insignia. As it is understood that the policy of G.H.Q., is not to have official insignia so much the alike as to lead to confusion, this matter is referred for consideration." Several exchanges of indorsement to the aforesaid communication were written with one citing that "the 79th Division is willing to share the cross with us…", and with the recommendation of approval from C.G. S.O.S. on 3 February 1919 by telegram G.H.Q., A.E.F. advised Commanding General, Advance Section, S.O.S. "M-250 Distinctive cloth design submitted by you approved this date." On same date by 5th Ind. to the aforesaid communication G.H.Q., A.E.F. wrote through Commanding General, S.O.S., To Commanding General, Advance Section, S.O.S. "In view of preceding indorsements, the distinctive insignia for Advanced Section, S.O.S., drawing of which appended hereto, is approved. Attention invited to attached copy of letter to Commanding General, 79th Division." Said letter of February 3, 1919 advised Commanding General, 79th division "Reference your letter of the 17th ult., regarding distinctive insignia for your Division and that of Advanced Section, S.O.S., it is not thought that there is enough similarity in these designs to cause confusion. The design selected by the Advanced Section, S.O.S., has been approved this date."

SERVICES OF SUPPLY – INTERMEDIATE SECTION GENERAL INTERMEDIATE
STORAGE DEPOT
Within the Services of Supply Intermediate Sector the General Intermediate Storage Depot
at Gièves, France, was the largest depot in the AEF with over 25,000 personnel.
SSI Approved: 11 June 1919

On 2 June 1919 Commanding Officer, Headquarters G.I.S.D. wrote Commanding
General S.O.S. "1. It is requested that a shoulder insignia as per inclosed drawing be
authorized for this command. The Diamond represents the diamond shape of the plant,
and the initials stand for the words "General Intermediate Storage Depot" The insignia
is to be of black cloth with letters embroidered in yellow." The letter further noted "3.
This command has been about equal in strength to that of a Division and has been of
that strength for over a year. A large number of officers and men have requested a special
insignia be authorized and I concur in that request." By 1st Ind. HQ.SOS to the C. in C., AEF
"Forwarded, recommending approval." On June 11, 1919, by 2nd Ind. G.H.Q., American
E.F. to Commanding General, S.O.S. "Approved."

Design drawing courtesy American Society of Military Insignia Collectors.

Sample from the collection of The Johnson Brothers.

REGULATING STATIONS AND RAILHEADS
SSI Approved: 16 January 1919

On 29 November 1918 Regulating Officer, American Regulating Station B, St. Dizier wrote Adjutant General, American E.F. "1. A symbol of identification to be worn by the personnel of this Regulating Station would facilitate the apprehension of the A.W.O.L.'s in this area. 2. Inclosed find sample symbol, approval of which is desired. DIMENSIONS Black background diagonals 4" – 2 1/2" and longest diagonal to be vertical. Gold letter R – width 1/2" and height 7/8" By 1ˢᵗ Ind. G.H.Q., American E.F. on 3 December 1918 to the Officer in Charge, Regulating Station, St. Dizier wrote "Disapproved; distinctive symbols are not authorized for Regulating Stations." In 2ⁿᵈ Ind. of 9 December R.O., St. Dizier wrote G-4, G.H.Q., American E.F. "1. It is requested that request for approval of symbol for Regulating Station be reconsidered as two-thirds of total personnel of this station is employed at railheads. 2. It is understood that the adoption of Divisional symbols was to facilitate the apprehension of absent without leave men; and, as, at each railhead, there are always numerous casuals and replacements lost or en route to divisions, it is considered that this symbol would assist the railhead officers in distinguishing those men on duty at the railheads from those who are assigned to other organizations. 3. At this station, there are approximately ninety men assigned to handling of casuals passing through the local casual camp; and it is considered that, if these men were allowed to adopt this symbol, it would expedite the handling of casuals, as the men on duty at the station would be easily recognized and, at the same time, would have a symbol which would carry a certain amount of authority to direct the handling of numerous detachments that are passing daily."

On 7 January 1919, Asst. Chief of Staff, G-4, GHQ., AEF wrote Chief of Staff, A.E.F. "1. It is requested that approval be granted for the personnel assigned to Regulating Stations and Railheads to wear the following arm insignia: Black diamond, 3 inches by 2 3/8 inches, device to be worn on left sleeve of coat and overcoat near the shoulder seam with long axis vertical. Device of Regulating station to have gold piping 3/12 in. wide. Device of personnel of Railheads to have red piping 3/32 in. wide. An R of block letter type having a line of 3/16 inches in width to be super imposed on the diamond. The R to be worn by the personnel of the Regulating Station and by the personnel of the Railheads served by that Regulating Station to be of the same color. The following to be the colors of the R's to be worn by the various stations. Is-sur-Tille Red Liffol-le- Grand White St. Dizier Blue Conflans Violet Treves Yellow Coblentz Green". On the copy of the document in the National Archives is noted "Approved 1/16/19". By 1ˢᵗ Ind. of 16 January 1919 G.H.Q., American E.F. to the Asst. chief of Staff, G-4 wrote "Approved."

On 19 January 1919 C. in C. by GHQ 4ᵗʰ Sec. wrote to Regulating Officer, St. Dizier. R. O., Treves. Regulating Officer, Is-sur-Tille. R. O., Coblents. Regulating Officer, Liffol-le-Grand. R. O., Conflans. "Subject: Army ensign for the Regulating Station and Railhead personnel. 1. The following arm insignia for the personnel assigned to Regulating Stations and Railhead has been approved: Black diamond, 3 inches by 2 3/8 inches, device to be worn on left sleeve of coat and overcoat near the shoulder seam with long axis vertical. Devise of Regulating Station to have gold piping 3/32 in. wide. Device of personnel of Railheads to have red piping 3/32 in. wide. An R of block letter type having a line of 3/16 inches in width to be super imposed on the diamond. The R to be worn by the personnel of the Regulating Station and by the personnel of the Railheads served by that Regulating Station to be of the same color. The following to be the colors of the R's to be worn by the various stations.

Is-sur-Tille	Red	Conflans Violet
Liffol-le-Grand	White	Treves Yellow
St. Dizier	Blue	Coblentz Green

2. You are authorized to make requisitions on Office of the Chief Quartermaster. A.E.F., at Tours, for the required supply."

As a "P.S. Attached will be found a sheet showing the various insignia."

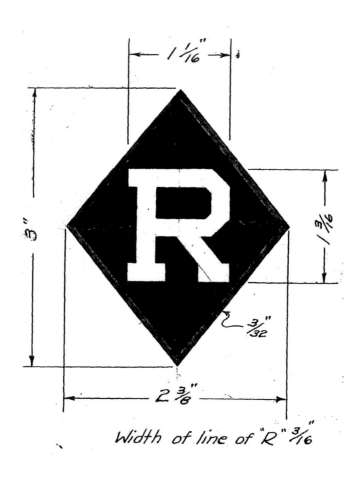

Design drawing attached to file copy of 16 January 1919 approval 1ˢᵗ Ind.. and believed to have been inclosed with 7 January 1919 communication of Asst. Chief of Staff, G-4, GHQ., AEF. to Chief of Staff, A.E.F.

Design drawing attached to 19 January 1919 communication of C in C to Regulating and Railhead Officers.

13ᵀᴴ ENGINEERS (RAILWAY)
Approved: 12 February 1919

On 11 February 1919 Commanding Officer, 13th Engineers (Railway), wrote Adjutant General, G.H.Q. American E. F. "1. The 13th Engineers, while in the service of the 2d French Army for a period of over fourteen months in the Verdun Sector were considered as a part of their combat forces and as such were fully armed at all times. During that period the 13th Engineers were practically isolated from the rest of the American forces until the St. Mihiel and Argonne-Meuse offensives. In view of the long service of this regiment, request is made for authority for its members to wear a shoulder insignia designed as follows: FIRST CHOICE: A square blue field with the engineer castle in red surrounded by a circle of thirteen stars; symbolical of the red, white and blue of our own colors; the blue, white and red of our ally, which they served, the thirteen stars denoting the thirteen original states whose united efforts founded our native land, and further that as they were the first states, so was this regiment the first in the service on the front and first in the Verdun sector. SECOND CHOICE: Blue, white and red; French colors, with the red castle superimposed, denoting service with the French and the arm of the service. THIRD CHOICE: Black diamond with numeral 13 in center on a white field." By telegram on 12 February 1919 G.H.Q., A.E.F. replied "M-305 period In view of fact 13th Engrs has never been part of any division, corps, or army, first choice of distinctive insignia submitted this date is approved." On February 19, 1919 General Headquarters American E.F. from the Adjutant General to Commanding Officer, 13 Engineers advised "The Commander-in-Chief directs that you furnish, with the least practicable delay, to Commanding General, S. O. S., a sample of the distinctive insignia authorized for your command with complete description and dimensions." On 27 February 1919 Commanding Officer wrote to Commanding General, S.O.S., American E. F. "1. Pursuant to instructions from the Adjutant General, G.H.Q., dated February 19th, 1919, a sample of the Distinctive Insignia authorized for this regiment attached herewith. Dimensions: Field of Blue, 2 1/2" square, a circle of thirteen 1/4" stars, two inches in diameter, enclosing a red castle, one inch base."

Design painting attached to 11 February 1919 communication of Commanding Officer, 13th Engineers to The Adjutant General, G.H.Q., A.E.F. and depicting the three noted choices. Choice 1 approved 12 February 1919.

POSTAL EXPRESS SERVICE AND OVERSEAS COURIERS
SSI Approved: 21 February 1919 (Overseas Couriers by War Department 5 May 1919)

On 11 February 1919 Chief Postal Express Service wrote Adjutant General G.H.Q. "1. It is requested that the annexed model be approved as the form of shoulder insignia for the personnel of the Postal Express Service, consisting of a representation of a silver gray hound on a dark blue back ground." A sample insignia with a white gray hound on a bright blue background was also attached in the National Archives file. By telegram 21 February 1919 from G.H.Q., A.E.F. to Chief, Postal Express Service advised "M-379 period Sample submitted as distinctive insignia for PES is approved"

Subsequently, on April 25, 1919, Colonel Wyllie of General Staff sent a "MEMORANDUM FOR THE CHIEF OF STAFF: Subject: Insignia for Overseas Curriers. In January, the Chief of Embarkation recommended the adoption of an insignia to be worn by overseas couriers on account of the assistance it would have been in arranging for transportation, getting the right of way and in promotion of esprit de corps in the courier service. This recommendation was disapproved. Since that time the various divisional insignias, worn on the point of the left shoulder, have been recognized and the Director of Purchases, Storage and Traffic now recommends that a similar type of insignia be adopted for the couriers. The A.E.F. has adopted one for use by the courier service in France, including those ordered from G.H.Q. to Washington. A sample is submitted herewith consisting of a silver greyhound on a blue background. It is recommended that this be approved for wear on the point of the left shoulder." The same date by MEMORANDUM FOR THE DIRECTOR OF PURCHASE, STORAGE AND TRAFFIC from Assistant to the Chief of Staff, Director of Operations wrote "The Secretary of War approves the sample insignia submitted herewith for use by the courier service, to be worn on the point of the left shoulder in the same place of divisional insignia by officers while acting as overseas couriers only." The notation "APPROVED: May 5 1919 By order of the Secretary of War" followed.

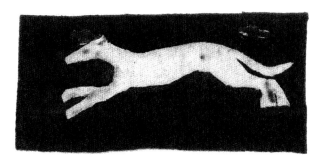

Sample annexed to 11 February 1919 communication of Chief, Postal Express Service to Adjutant General and approved 21 February 1919.

LIAISON SERVICE
SSI Approved: 4 April 1919

On 3 April 1919 Chief Liaison Officer wrote The Adjutant General, A.E.F., G.H.Q., A.E.F. "1. Authorization is hereby requested for the Liaison Service to wear the enclosed shoulder insignia." In a letter from Chief Liaison Service of 3 April 1919 to Lieutenant Colonel James Jones, A.G. Personnel Dept. Adjutant General's Office, G.H.Q., A.E.F. accompanying the request for authorization of the insignia wrote "In our selection of the insignia, we have endeavored to emphasize the idea of liaison with the French, by adopting half of the French Staff insignia on a "bleu horizon" background. For your information, the French Authorities, at the Ministry of War, have given their approval. As all Liaison Officers found in Paris after April 5th. without the "Fleur-de-lys" insignia, are liable to disciplinary action, I would greatly appreciate it if it were possible to secure the approval of the Adjutant General for this new insignia, practically at once. I will therefore take the liberty of calling you up to-morrow afternoon, in hope of securing a favorable answer." By 1st Ind. of 4 April 1919 G.H.Q. , American E.F. to Chief Liaison Officer, American E.F. "Approved."

Sketch based on description.

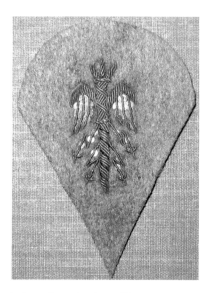

Sample from the collection of The Johnson Brothers.

CENTRAL RECORDS OFFICE – ADJUTANT GENERAL'S DEPARTMENT
SSI Approved: 27 January 1919

Central Records Office, Adjutant General's Department, American Ex. Forces prepared a "WRAPPER" including a drawing of the "Diagram of suggested emblem for the Central Records Office, Adjutant General's Department, American Ex. Forces." By 1st Ind. of 25 January 1919 Central Records Office, A.G. Dept., to the Adjutant General, G.H.Q., A.E.F. forwarded the design "requesting approval and that same be registered." By telegram of 27 January 1919 G.H.Q., A.E.F. advised Officer in Charge, Central Records Office BOURGES "M-206. Distinctive insignia submitted for CRO of golden eagle mounted on AGD shield red, white and blue is approved."

Sample from the collection of The Johnson Brothers.

A- BLACK BACKGROUND
B- GOLD EAGLE
C - SILVER STARS
D - SHIELD OF COLORS SHOWN IN DIAGRAM.
E - STARS TO SAME AS-A.G.D.- SHIELD

Design drawing ("WRAPPER" - reduced) inclosed with 25 January 1919 1st Ind. of Central Records Office, A.G. Dept. and approved by 17 January 1919 telegram M-206.

AMBULANCE SERVICE
SSI Approved: 5 January 1919

On 21 December, Medical Corps Chief of Service wrote Adjutant General, G.H.Q., American E.F. "1. Authority is requested for the members of this Service to wear on the left shoulder a distinctive insignia to differentiate them from the personnel of either Medical Department organizations of the American E.F. 2. The insignia contemplated for the members of this Service, a model of which is inclosed, will consist of the figure of a cock in white, superimposed upon a circular background of maroon. In view of the fact that maroon is the color of the Medical Department and the cock the emblem of the Republic of France, this emblem is considered an appropriate insignia for this branch of the Medical Department on duty with the French Army. encl.1." by 1st Ind. by G.H.Q., American E.F. on 27 December 1918 to C.O., U.S. Ambulance Service with French Army advised "Disapproved. Distinctive insignia is only authorized for divisional, corps, and army troops, Base Sections and G.H.Q. troops." By telegram from G.H.Q., A.E.F. of 5 January 1919 to Chief, U.S. Army Ambulance Service, Paris advised "M-41. Upon reconsideration distinctive insignia recommended by your letter of twenty first ultimo is approved. Please mail sample of design." (No further information or design was found in the file of the National Archives, although a painting of the design in the records of The Institute of Heraldry depicts a white Gallic rooster on a red disc.)

Design painting from the records of The Institute of Heraldry.

CAMP PONTANEZEN
SSI Approved: 7 May 1919

On 28 April 1919 Commanding General, Camp Pontanezen, Base Section No. 5, S.O.S., wrote Commanding General, Base Section No. 5, S.O.S. "1. A Board of Officers was convened by the C. G. of Camp Pontanezen for the purpose of suggesting a design as might be appropriate for the personnel of Camp Pontanezen. 2. The Board found that the "Duckboard design" would be most appropriate and it is therefore recommended that it be authorized." By 3rd Ind of 7 May 1919 from G.H.Q., American E.F. to Commanding General, S.O.S. advised "Approved. In view of the large number of troops as this Camp and the arduous nature of their duties, a special exception is made in this case. This will not, however, be considered a precedent for other Base Sections or Ports of the S.O.S."

Design painting from the records
of The Institute of Heraldry.

Sample from the collection of The Johnson Brothers.

CHEMICAL WARFARE SERVICE
SSI Approved: 18 January 1919

On 16 January 1919 GHQ, AEF, Office C.W.S. Rep. 4th Sec. G.S. wrote a Memorandum for the Adjutant General: "1. In the near future there will be several detachments of the Chemical Warfare Service operating with the 1st Army in carrying on demonstrations in the offensive use of chemical warfare materials in connection with certain tactical problems to be carried out as part of the training schedule. If this work is considered valuable it is the intention to extend the training to other Armies. 2. In order that the special troops carrying on this work may be distinguished readily by the officers of the Chemical Warfare Service as well as by officers of other arms, who may desire to question them on various operations, it is requested that authority be granted for the members of the demonstrating parties of the Chemical Warfare Service to wear the attached shield, made up of the two colors cobalt blue and chrome yellow, which are the official colors of the Chemical Warfare Service." On 18 January 1919 the Adjutant General replied "Distinctive cloth insignia to be worn by members of the Chemical Warfare Service submitted with your memorandum of January 16, 1919, is approved." Also a 1st Ind. from Office Chief of Chemical Warfare Service, HQ, S.O.S. dated 27 Feb. 1918 (note date error 1918 vs. 1919) to the Adjutant General stated "1. Returned. Enclosed sample of the distinctive insignia authorized for the Chemical Warfare Service, size, approximately 2 ½ inches by 2 ½ inches, colors, cobalt blue on the upper half and chrome yellow on the lower half."

Design painting from the records of The Institute of Heraldry.

Sample from the author's collection.

DISTRICT OF PARIS
SSI Approved: 11 March 1919

On 15 February 1919 HEADQUARTERS, DISTRICT OF PARIS issued General Order No. 2 as follows: "1. A District of Paris insignia has been approved and will be worn by all Officers, Enlisted Men and other ranks of the United Sates Army on duty in the District of Paris. The wearing of this insignia is compulsory and Organization Commanders will be held responsible for its proper use by the members of their organizations. 2. SPECIFICATIONS: FOR OFFICERS. Black Broadcloth Triangle with Silver Gray Fleur de Lis of silver thread in the center. Triangle to measure "3 ¼" across the base and "4 ¼" on the sides and to be worn base up on the left arm with the base line flush with the top of the sleeve where it joins the shoulder of the blouse. FOR ENLISTED MEN, Black Broadcloth with Silver Gray Fleur de Lis of same material in the center. Dimensions same as for Officers. ..." On 5 March 1919 HEADQUARTERS, DISTRICT OF PARIS issued GENERAL ORDERS No 3 as follows: "I. General Orders No. 2, Hqs. District of Paris, dated February 15th, 1919, is hereby revoked. II. 1. A District of Paris insignia has been approved and will be worn by all Officers, Enlisted Men and other ranks of the United States Army on duty in the District of Paris. The wearing of this insignia is compulsory and Organization Commanders will be held responsible for its proper use by members of their organizations. This insignia may be worn by army nurses and militarized civilians on duty in this command. 2. SPECIFICATIONS: FOR OFFICERS: Black Broadcloth Triangle with Silver Gray Fleur de Lis of silver thread in the center. Triangle to measure 3 1/4" across base line flush with top of the sleeve where it joins the shoulder of the blouse. FOR ENLISTED MEN: Black Broadcloth with Silver Gray Fleur de Lis of same material in the center. Dimensions same as for officers. ...III. When any member of the A.E.F., is relieved from duty with any Army, Corps or Division his authority to wear the insignia of that Army, Corps or Division ceases. IV. Members of the A.E.F. with the American Peace Commission will not wear the insignia authorized for the District of Paris." Subsequent indorsements 2, 3 and 4 recommended approval and in the 3rd Ind. of 3 March 1919 by Hq. Dist. of Paris it noted "1. A distinctive insignia for the Dist. of Paris was approved verbally by the C.G., SOS, prior to the issue of G.O. 2, Headquarters, Dist. of Paris, 15 Feb. 19 and is authorized by I. G. O.7, Headquarters SOS 6 Feb. 19. The manufacture and supply of the insignia to enlisted men has been approved by the Chief Q.M.A.E.F. ... 5. The distinctive insignias for the Dis. of Paris and the Peace Commission were adopted after conference with the C. G., SOS, as a police and disciplinary measure to readily distinguish the members of the A.E.F. resident in Paris from those visiting it. This plan, with the approval of the C.G. SOS, has been extended to include all motor transportation that a better appearance may be enforced in conformance with G.O. 12, SOS, 1919. 6. In case authority for the distinctive Dist. of Paris and Peace Commission Insignia has not been granted by the C. in C. such action is requested." By 5th Ind. of 11 March G. Hq., A. E. F., to Commanding General, S.O.S. wrote "1. In view of the fact that the Chief Quartermaster has started manufacture of the insignia for the Dist. of Paris, and that the Commanding General, S. O. S. recommends approval, it is herewith authorized. 2. As no design for a Peace Conference insignia has been received at there Headquarters, no action looking to approve of that can as yet be taken. The Commanding General, Troops in Paris, will be instructed that so much of his

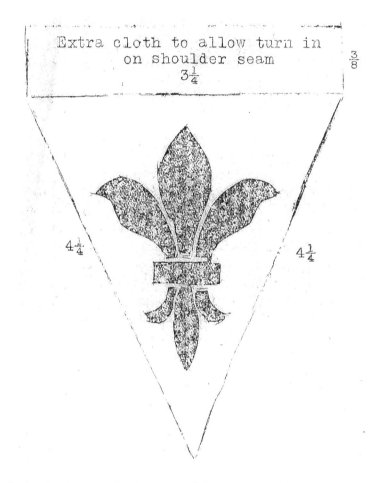

Design drawing inclosed with 6 March 1919 4th Ind. of Hq. S.O.S. to G.H.Q. A.E.F.

orders as makes compulsory the wearing of this insignia by officers and enlisted men, stationed in Paris, of services for whom a special insignia has been approved (such as the Postal Express Service) will be revoked. The Chief Quartermaster should be informed that, before he contracts for the manufacture and supply of any insignia, he should ascertain if same is authorized; and the attention of all concerned should be invited to the fact that authorization of any arm insignia can only be made by there headquarters."

Sample from the collection
of The Johnson Brothers.

NORTH RUSSIA EXPEDITIONARY FORCE
SSI Approved: 5 June 1919

On 5 June 1919 by telegram Commanding General, Expeditionary Force of North Russia to G.H.Q., A.E.F. wrote: "CO 559 JUNE 3 REQUEST AUTHORIZATION OF DESIGN FOR SHOULDER INSIGNIA FOR THIS EXPEDITION AS FOLLOWS COMMA WHITE POLAR BEAR ON BLUE FIELD – RICHARDSON -". On same date by telegram from G.H.Q., A.E.F. to Commanding General, U.S. Troops, ARCHANGEL replied: "M-1145 period Distinctive cloth insignia recommended by you is approved." On 11 June 1919 HEADQUARTERS AMERICAN EXPEDITIONARY FORCES NORTH RUSSA issued GENERAL ORDERS No. 5 "1. A white polar bear on a blue field has been authorized by G.H.Q., A.E.F. telegram dated 5 June 1919 as the insignia for the A. E. F. in North Russia. 2. This insignia will be made on cloth and sewn on the left sleeve of the blouse and overcoat 1 inch below the shoulder seam. It will be worn by all Officers and enlisted men of this command. 3. The Quartermaster will provide and issue the necessary number of insignia to all organizations."
(From the records of the National Archives.)

Sample from the records of the National Archives.

TANK CORPS
SSI Approved: 30 January 1919

On 19 December 1918 General Headquarters, Tank Corps, American Expeditionary Forces issued GENERAL ORDERS No. 25 "1. In order to comply with the requirements of the various Armies that all Officers and Soldiers in their areas be plainly marked with appropriate insignia the following distinctive insignia has been adopted for Tank Corps troops, American Expeditionary Forces. This insignia will be worn only on the left sleeve of coat, overcoat, raincoat, trench coat, and olive drab shirt, when blouse is not worn, with yellow tip 1 inch from the shoulder seam of sleeve of coat, red point being to the front and the red-blue edge horizontal. This insignia will be of suitable heavy cloth, in colors and size as follows: (The insignia is depicted indicating 2.5" Sides and colors Cavalry Yellow, Artillery Red and Infantry Blue.) 2. These Headquarters will take the necessary steps to secure these insignia from the Quartermaster's Department for all Tank Corps troops, American Expeditionary Forces, and, as soon as the necessary supply has been obtained, will distribute the requisite number to each Tank Corps unit. 3. Hereafter no distinctive insignia other than the one dictated in paragraph 1 of this order will be worn by any Tank Corps troops, American Expeditionary Forces. By command of Brigadier General ROCKENBACH." On 30 January 1919 G.H.Q., A.E.F. advised Chief of Tank Corps, A.E.F. "Approved".

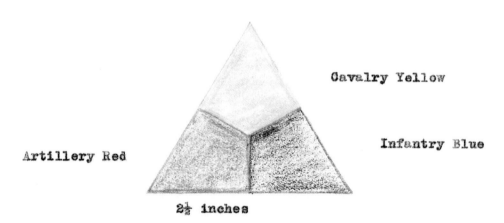

Design depicted on 17 December 1918 GENERAL ORDERS No. 25
of General Headquarters, Tank Corps.

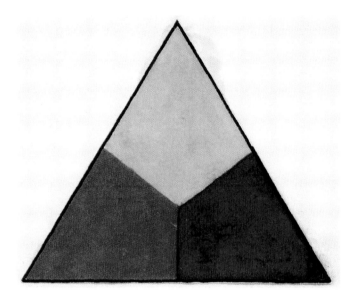

Design painting from the records of the National Archives.

SECOND CORPS SCHOOLS
SSI Approved: 18 January 1919

On 18 December 1918 Commandant, 2ⁿᵈ Corps Schools, wrote Asst. Chief of Staff, G-5, G.H.Q., A.E.F. "SUBJECT: Distinguishing badge. 1. Authority is requested for the Instructors and Assistant Instructors at these Schools to wear a distinguishing badge in the manner and of the general shape of those now used by divisions. 2. This is made necessary by the fact that at the present time it is impossible for the students to recognize the instructors. An attempt was made to use an arm band which was not permanently attached to the coat. This was unsatisfactory because of being lost and presenting an untidy appearance. 3. With the number of students which the School will have in future and the fact that all students are combined for Tactical work in the afternoon, in which the Instructors and Assistant instructors participate, it is necessary that they have some defining mark whereby students may recognize the authority which they have to issue orders and instructions in connection with the exercise. 4. A suggested design is submitted herewith. Request that action on this matter be expedited." On 23 December 1918 A. C. of S., G-5 sent a "MEMORANDUM FOR Chief of Staff 1. It is requested that authority be granted to the Commandant, his staff, instructors, and assistant instructors, of the 2ⁿᵈ and 3ʳᵈ Corps Schools, to wear, as is now worn by divisions, an insignia of the pattern shown herewith, for the reasons as stated in the inclosed communication." It is believed the inclosure was the same as that with the 18 December 1918 communication noted above. By 1ˢᵗ Ind. of 23 December 1918 G.H.Q., A.E.F. to Commandant, 2ⁿᵈ Corps Schools replied "Returned. Approved. 1. Copy of design, as soon as finished, will be furnished these headquarters for file." On 25 December 1918 the Adjutant General wrote "MEMORANDUM FOR THE CHIEF OF STAFF: Present instructions from the Chief of Staff, only authorize distinctive insignia for Divisions, Armies and Corps and personnel of G.H.Q. and Sections of the S.O.S. Inasmuch as the insignia requested herein is very similar to that authorized for the 30ᵗʰ Division, approval of this particular insignia is not recommended." Attached to the memorandum is the proposed design showing a red disc with blue outer circle and blue Roman numerals II and III respectively in a vertical position. Subsequently, a revised design was submitted depicting a white disc with a red outer border and the numerals 2 and 3 respectively and letters C S in blue. On 18 January 1919 the Adjutant General wrote "Memorandum for the Asst. Chief of Staff, G-5: The Commander-in-Chief directs me to inform you that the distinctive cloth insignias submitted for the 2ⁿᵈ and 3ʳᵈ Corps schools are approved." On 21 January 1919 the Adjutant General wrote Commandant, 2ⁿᵈ Corps School. "Subject Distinctive Insignia. The inclosed design has been approved as the distinctive insignia for the 2ⁿᵈ Corps Schools." The attached inclosure depicts the 2ⁿᵈ and 3ʳᵈ Corps Schools insignia.

Note: On 24 February 1919 Director, 2ⁿᵈ Corps Engineering School To: COMMANDANT, 2ⁿᵈ Corps Schools wrote "1. There is submitted herewith a true copy of the approved insignia of the Second Corps Schools, description of which follows: "3/16" Vermillon band on white field 2 3/4" in diameter. Large numeral (2) 1 1/2" high with small letters C & S, all in blue significant of 2ⁿᵈ Corps schools."

Large numeral (2) 1 1/2" high with small letters C & S, all in blue significant of 2ⁿᵈ Corps." The noted designs of both 2ⁿᵈ and 3ʳᵈ Corps Schools were attached.

Design drawing as approved 18 January 1919.

THIRD CORPS SCHOOLS
SSI Approved: 18 January 1919

Although the records did not reveal the request from Commandant, 3rd Corps Schools, it is evident that the correspondence relating to the designs and approval were applicable to both 2nd and 3rd Corps Schools. Subsequent to the approval of 18 January 1918, on 21 January 1919 the Adjutant General wrote Commandant, 3rd Corps School. "Subject Distinctive Insignia. The inclosed design has been approved as the distinctive insignia for the 3rd Corps Schools." The attached inclosure depicts the 2nd and 3rd Corps School insignia. On 27 January 1919 the Adjutant, Third Corps Schools wrote "MEMORANDUM No. 12 Extract Par. 2. Par. 1 Memorandum No. 8, these Headquarters, dated January 20th, 1919, authorizing a distinctive insignia to be worn by all soldiers of the Third Corps Schools, is hereby revoked. Par. 3. Soldiers of this command who are wearing the insignia authorized by Par. 1. Memorandum No. 8, these Headquarters, will immediately remove same. An insignia authorized by General Headquarters, American Expeditionary Forces, will take the place of the insignia authorized by the above memorandum, and will be issued by the Quartermaster in the near future. This memorandum will be published on all bulletin boards, and will be read to all soldiers of the Third Corps Schools at three formations." It is believed this memorandum was to clarify that the insignia submitted 18 December 1918 was not that approved by G.H.Q., A.E.F. 18 January 1919.

Design drawing as approved 18 January 1919.

Design drawing on 21 January 1919 approval of G.H.Q., A.E.F.

EDUCATIONAL CORPS – AMERICAN E. F. UNIVERSITY
SSI Approved 18 April 1919

On 2 March 1919 A.C. of S., G-5 by MEMORANDUM wrote Chief of Staff "1. It is believed that an insignia to be worn on the left arm in the usual manner by the officials of the A. E. F. University and officers and soldiers attending as students, will do much towards creating an esprit de corps for that institution and will also be an aid to discipline as it affords a means of distinguishing at once, students from other officers and soldiers on duty at the University. 2. The design for students (officers and soldiers) will be stamped out of felt and can be provided at small cost. The design for officials of the University (officers' insignia) will be embroidered and will be purchased by such individual officer. 3. The approval of there insignia, as per attached designs, is requested." A drawing with the insignia depicted was attached. In reply by 1ˢᵗ Ind. of 3 March Chief of Staff, GHQ, AEF replied to A.C.S. G-5, G.H.Q. "Returned. – Officers and soldiers are on detached service while at the University, - that is they still belong to a unit and should wear the Arm Insignia of that unit. The proposal of the above memorandum is therefore disapproved."

On 10 April 1919 HEADQUARTERS AMERICAN E. F. UNIVERSITY issued MEMORANDUN No. 29 "1. The following design for arm insignia for members of Educational Corps, having received official approval from G. H. Q., is published for information and guidance of all concerned. This design is to be worn on the right sleeve in manner similar to that in which Army, Corps and Divisional insignia is worn on the left sleeve by members of the Army. The dimensions indicated are in inches. The same insignia will be worn on the right side of cap. A bronze ornament for the collar has been designed and will be secured at an early date. (Sketch of design depicted on memorandum.) 2. The above insignia will be substituted for present insignia on April 16, 1919." On 18 April 1919 G.H.Q., A.E.F. advised President, A. E. F. University by telegram "Number 6697 G-5 period Insignia per your memorandum twenty nine approved period Order will be issued covering same authorizing it on sleeves and one approximately one half size on overseas cap period Direct your quartermaster obtain one thousand large size and five hundred small size for sale members Educational Corps".

Sample from the collection
of The Johnson Brothers.

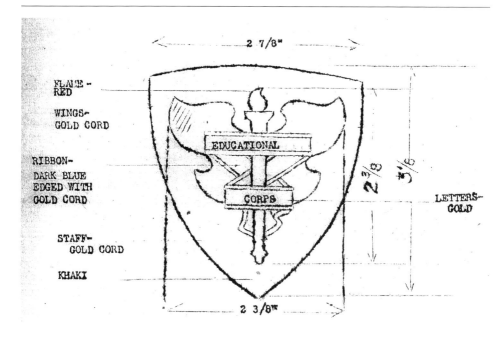

Design drawing depicted on Headquarters, American E.F. University
10 April 1919 Memorandum, No. 29.

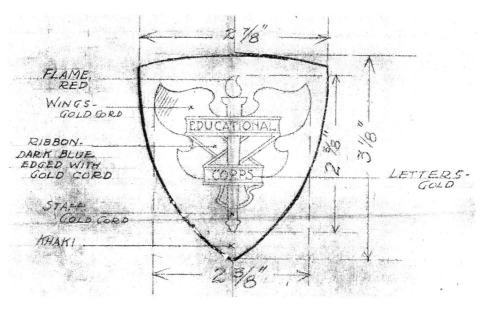

Design drawing from the records of the National Archives.

FOURTH MARINE BRIGADE
LINEAGE
Constituted 23 October 1917 in France. 8 August 1919 transferred to naval service.
CAMPAIGN PARTICIPATION CREDIT
World War I
Aisne
Aisne-Marne
St. Mihiel
Meuse-Argonne
See 2nd Division

FIFTH MARINE BRIGADE
LINEAGE
Constituted 5 September 1918. Organized 15 September 1918 at Marine barracks, Quantico, Virginia. Demobilized 13 August 1919 at Marine barracks Quantico, Virginia.
CAMPAIGN PARTICIPATION CREDIT
NONE
SSI Approved: 20 June 1919

On 2 June 1919 Commanding General, 5ᵗʰ Marine Brigade, wrote The Commander in Chief, G.H.Q., A.E.F. "1. It is recommended that the following shoulder insignia be authorized for the 5ᵗʰ Brigade, U.S. Marines.

BRIGADE HEADQUARTERS:
Insignia crimson circular shield with black device and gold-yellow Roman "V". Note: The gold is taken to represent gold lace and represents the highest rank of the unit and the gold numeral is retained in different shaped squares, for Headquarters of the several Regiments.

MACHINE GUN BATTALION:
Crimson circular shield and purple numeral "V". Note: The purple figure has been adopted as distinctive for Machine Gun units and the same numeral is used in the square field for the Machine Gun Companies of the several Regiments.

HEADQUARTERS AND HEADQUARTERS COMPANY, SENIOR REGIMENT (11ᵗʰ Regt)
See remarks with regard to Brigade Headquarters. Square shield, black device and gold-yellow numeral "V". Shape of backing indicates regiment and color of the Roman "V" indicates Headquarters. The Headquarters Company naturally uses the same colored numeral.

MACHINE GUN COMPANY, SENIOR REGIMENT (11ᵗʰ Regt)
Indicated by shape of the backing and by the purple Roman numeral.

SUPPLY COMPANY, SENIOR REGIMENT (11ᵗʰ Regt)
This company is indicated by green Roman figure which has been adopted for the Supply Companies.

BATTALION INSIGNIA
The color schemes of red, white and blue, our National colors, are used for the designation of the several battalions.
The senior regiment, as already stated, is indicated by the square crimson field, and the First Battalion is shown by the crimson numeral; the Second Battalion has by the white, and the Third Battalion by the blue.

The same scheme is used with regard to the junior Regiment (13th Regiment). The square has been turned on end, and the same markings, company for company, and battalion for battalion, are used.

2. Attached hereto is a copy of the proposed insignia for Brigade Headquarters, others to be varied as indicated."

By 1st Ind. of 4 June Hqrs. Base Section No. 5, S.O.S. to C.G., S.O.S. wrote "1. Forwarded, recommending approval." By 2nd Ind. of 12 June 1919 Hdqrs.. S.O.S. to C-in-C, American E.F. wrote "1. Forwarded, recommending approval, to take effect when 5th Brigade is concentrated as a unit." On 20 June by 3rd Ind. G.H.Q., American E.F. to Commanding General, S. O. S. wrote "Approved as recommended in 2nd indorsement." On 23 June Hdqrs., S. O. S. to C. G., Base Section #5, S. O. S. wrote "1 Attention is invited to 2nd Indorsement, and the approval thereof. 2 The insignia will not be distributed nor worn until the 5th Marine Brigade is concentrated as a unit."

Symbolism: Marine Corps eagle, globe, and anchor with Roman numeral "V" to represent the Fifth Marine Brigade.

Sketch based on description. Fifth Marine Brigade, Headquarters with gold-yellow "V" Machine Gun Battalion with purple "V".

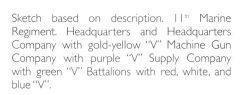

Sketch based on description. 11th Marine Regiment. Headquarters and Headquarters Company with gold-yellow "V" Machine Gun Company with purple "V" Supply Company with green "V" Battalions with red, white, and blue "V".

Sketch based on description. 13ᵗʰ Marine Regiment. Headquarters and Headquarters Company with gold-yellow "V". Machine Gun Company with purple "V". Supply Company with green "V". Battalions with red, white, and blue "V".

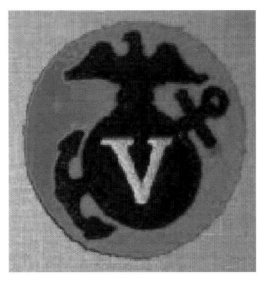

Sample from the collection of The Johnson Brothers. Fifth Marine Brigade, Machine Gun Battalion.

Sample from the collection of The Johnson Brothers. 11th Marine Regiment, Headquarters and Headquarters Company.

Sample from the collection of The Johnson Brothers. 13th Marine Regiment, Headquarters and Headquarters Company.

On 23 January 1919 the Post Commander, Marine Barracks, Quantico, VA, wrote the Major General Commandant:

"Subject: Division Identification Marks.

1. During the past month, a large number of men have returned to this post from overseas. When they arrived here, they were nearly all wearing, in addition to the decorations which they had presumably received abroad, the identification mark of the Second Division, on the left shoulder.

2. This Second Division badge consists of a red circle, 3 ¾ inches in diameter; having in its center a white circle of 2 inches in diameter; on this is superimposed a five-pointed blue star, having stitched to its center an Indian head.

3. Upon arrival here, the men were furnished with clean Marine Corps uniforms, in exchange for the battle-worn Army garments, and it has been noted that the men immediately procure these division marks and have them sewed to their new uniforms. While the Post Commander knows of no Marine Corps order or regulation which authorizes the wearing of these marks, he has refrained from issuing any orders prohibiting the same, on account of the evident pride with which the men display this mark of their service overseas.

4. In view of the fact of the apparent desire of men returning from foreign service, who have served in the Second Division, to wear some outward visible sign of that service, it is recommended that an order be issued authorizing the wearing of these distinguishing marks by any individual who has served in the Second Division overseas, in battle, for as long a time as he may remain in the United States Marine Corps. It is believed that the wearing of this distinguishing mark will tend to keep alive the traditions of the great war, wherein the members of this Corps so greatly distinguished themselves. Men who wear this badge will be pointed out, in years to come, as active participants in this great adventure, and the explanation of the meaning of the badge should never fail to arouse interest among recruits or among the civilian population."

In reply of 5 February 1919 Major General Commandant advised "In order that units of the Marines returning from service abroad may follow the same procedure as that prescribed for the Army with reference to the wearing of divisional insignia, etc., War Department Circular No. 42, dated January 25, 1919, is quoted for the information and guidance of all officers and men concerned:

1. War Department Circular No. 42, dated January 25, 1919, on the subject of "Divisional Insignia", provides as follows: Circular No. 18, War Department, 1919, is rescinded and the following substituted therefore:

Officers and enlisted men returning from France as casuals for the purpose of discharge, will be permitted to wear insignia indicating the tactical division, Army Corps or Army with which they served overseas. This applies not only to those who are to be immediately discharged but also to those reatined in hospitals pending discharge.

Officers and enlisted men returning as casuals not for discharge but for active duty in this country will be required to remove such insignia.

Units returning from overseas for the purpose of demobilization will be permitted to wear divisional, Army corps or Army insignia until demobilized. Units returning for station in this country, which are not to be demobilized will be required to remove such insignia."